SONGS
FROM THE OTHER
SIDE

DISCOVERING GOD'S WONDER
AND HEAVEN'S WORSHIP SONGS

LAMAR BOSCHMAN

WORSHIP
INSTITUTE.COM®

WorshipInstitute.com Publishing

Published by WorshipInstitute.com Publishing
P.O. Box 130 Bedford, TX 56095

ISBN 0-9759165-0-5

Printed in the United States of America

PREFACE

"LaMar Boschman's characteristic biblical wisdom, spiritual insight
and clear-eyed good sense are in hand once again, here in his book
"Songs from the Other Side." What makes his work so accessible and
practical is his deep and genuine love for the Savior as it joins
to his passionate pursuit of a lifestyle of worship."

- Jack Hayford -
King's College and Seminary, Los Angeles, CA

"Our culture cries for the transcendent, for that something of 'heaven'
to break into our days. In Songs from the Other Side, LaMar
Boschman has articulated the issue precisely: the secret of life is not in
getting God to come to us, but in us getting to that 'realm' in which He
abides. With both passion and eloquence, the author describes that
'realm,' then bids us enter. What awaits the reader is a worship
journey that leads not only to that which most satisfies the heart - the
Presence of God - but that which will permanently arrest the
imagination: the grandeur of the Throne Room. Here we are invited to
encounter God's expressions of His own wonder, and then allow those
sounds and songs of heaven to penetrate our present."

- Steve Fry -
Pastor Belmont Church, Nashville, TN

TABLE OF CONTENTS

SONGS FROM THE OTHER SIDE

THE ALIEN ANTHEM
(Revelation 4:8)

Holy, holy, holy,
Lord God Almighty,
Who was and is and is to come!

———————

THE CREATION CANTICLE
(Revelation 4:11)

You are worthy, O Lord,
To receive glory and honor and power;
For You created all things,
And by Your will they exist and were created.

———————

THE SONG OF REDEMPTION
(Revelation 5:9, 10)

You are worthy to take the scroll,
And to open its seals;
For You were slain,
And have redeemed us to God by Your blood
Out of every tribe and tongue and people and nation.
And have made us kings and priests to our God;
And we shall reign on the earth.

THE ANGEL ANTHEM
(Revelation 5:12)

Worthy is the Lamb who was slain
To receive power and riches and wisdom,
And strength and honor and glory and blessing!

CREATION'S CRESCENDO
(Revelation 5:13)

Blessing and honor and glory and power
Be to Him who sits on the throne,
And to the Lamb, forever and ever!

CHAPTER ONE

LOOK UP

Transcendent worship is that which goes beyond human experience and involves the eternal.

Imagine…a man is ascending a narrow mountain road. He is tired and hot and thirsty. His breathing is shallow and labored because the air is getting thin. As he stops to rest, he hears a faint, distant roar through the silence of the moment. Could it be the sound of running water? Following the noise, he leaves the road and plows through a mile of dense grass and shrubs. He climbs over and around boulders. The way is hard, but he presses on. The roar is loud now and much more distinct. Peering through the vegetation, he stops to catch his breath!

Right there before him is a shimmering, beautiful mountain river, cascading over rocks and gathering in a broad, shady basin below. He stands stunned on a bluff as he watches the clear waters continue their sparkling tumble down the verdant mountainside.

Filled with delight, he leaps skyward and gracefully slices the surface; *ah, the cool depths of the refreshing waters!* For hours, he frolics, drinks deeply, dives and floats in the waters. The water is so crystal clear that he can see his feet and the colorful pebbles on the bottom. Then he reclines in the cool grass at the edge of this highland oasis. He's never found such a place.

After a while, the man begins to think of others who might be hot and tired and thirsty. He makes his way back to the road and scrawls "water: this way →" on a piece of bark with his knife. Using his shoelace, he ties his homemade sign to a tree in plain sight for other weary travelers.

Soon, other exhausted climbers find this special worshipful place. Before long, there are RVs, motorcycles, tents, and porta-potties. A whole community develops around this pristine pool of refreshment and beauty. Then, someone realizes that the "sound of many waters" can be recorded. Videotaped. Oh, the possibilities! *We can add some reverb, background singers, Dolby noise reduction, and digital enhancement.*

Artists begin to "interpret" the sights and sounds of the river and its pool. Camera platforms are constructed. Recording studios spring up like wildflowers. The bluff becomes hot real estate. The

Goodyear blimp hovers overhead. Wall Street takes notice, and slick travel magazines beckon the masses to this glamorous spot.

So gradually that no one notices, pollution becomes a problem and things start to float in the water. For no reason, fights break out and marriages break down. The water begins to taste funny. The pristine place is no longer what it was.

As a pioneer who has seen this happen to the waters of worship, I complained to the Lord. His response was, "Stop complaining and go farther up the mountain, closer to the Source, where the air is clear and the water runs pure. Come up to where I am." So I began to look up.

SEARCHING

I've been hungry for a higher level of worship. I believe this heart cry is a precursor to a coming spiritual earthquake in our worship experience. The Lord wants to break through the crust of our old, frozen patterns of worship and free us. There is developing in each of us an appetite for the transcendent that goes above the average, the mundane, the usual, and the ordinary! We are on the verge of God doing something tremendous among us through our worship of Him.

But in what direction do we look?

Where's the pattern for real worship?

Where can we look for more?

Where can we find worship that is pure and true?

The answer is simple, yet profound: *The pure and transcendent worship is fundamental and timeless.* It is in another dimension, a higher place. It's centered in Christ and the Christ event. For that, we look to His eternal Word. We look for records of those who saw the worship on the other side.

THE X FILES

The book of Revelation is a disclosure of Jesus Christ and the worship of Him. It reveals what worship is really like in the eternal realm. There, worship is more real and truer than what we have on this side.

> *Many times I have sat at my computer and typed with tears on my cheeks as I saw into the worship of heaven.*

As I studied five songs[1] of extra-celestials found in Revelation (known also as the Apocalypse), the Lord grabbed my heart. These magnificent creatures in heaven worship God as they sing of the slain Lamb. They sing of the One who is worthy. They sing of the Creator. They sing about the redemption provided by Christ. Their worship is unpolluted and glorious.

I have been overwhelmed by what I saw. Many times I have sat at my computer and typed with tears on my cheeks as I saw into the worship of heaven. What was revealed took my breath away. There is another realm and another possibility, which is what I call the "X-files" principle. There is something more out there to experience beyond our current perception. I am hungry for the transcendence of the worship music on the other side. Let it be done on earth as it is in heaven. Come into God's presence with heaven's music.

BARNACLES & BOATS

Our modern-day culture has complicated worship. We have downloaded, digitized, and driven our worship with technology. We have pumped-up, hyped-up, pre-formed, pre-fabricated our worship with glam and glitz trying to make it more appealing. We have settled for the sensational, the trendy, the mass-marketed and the "latest" in our worship. We have become so enamored with new gadgets and the latest thing that we forget that worship is for *God*—not for us. While there is nothing innately wrong with using quality technology and the newest things, these things should never distract us from what true worship is all about.

Our best artistic productions are just sounding brass and clanging cymbals if we have no internal heart attitude of worship.

Sometimes our worship doesn't look like worship anymore. American Christian culture has grown up around the way we worship like barnacles on a boat. Barnacles are not *the* boat; they are only *part of* the boat. We see the barnacles before we see the boat. Now you can tell what group people come from by how they dress, talk, sing, and act. In some cases people find their identity in the barnacles and not the boat.

We have added a bunch of extra "stuff" to our worship so that it's become an unreal experience. Perhaps that is why when many prisoners get out of jail, they say they don't want to go to church services because it's too plastic and phony. They actually desire to go back to the real worship they experienced in jail where everyone knows each other and there is no pretense. What's up with that?

THE THRILL IS GONE, BABY!

Many people in our pop-culture cannot find stability amid the constant tempest of turmoil and trouble. To them God may be nothing more than a "genie in a bottle" or a "feel-good." Many Christians come to church and sing songs to get a thrill, to have an experience or to just feel better about themselves. Why do I know this? Listen to what people say after services:

"What was the matter with the worship today?"

"I didn't get anything out of it!"

Comments like these tell me the people didn't worship. They didn't understand that worship is for God. Worship is for His eyes only, His ears only.

Consider that the reason why our worship is low today is because we have a low view of worship. Often our worship is a stimulation of sights and sounds for our pleasure. It's more sensual than we want to admit. It is consumer driven, people-centered and has the goal of creating a "feel-good." While this kind of "worship" seems fulfilling at the moment, it is not genuine and leaves us feeling empty. True worship found in the Scriptures transcends our current circumstances and ushers us into the presence of God. It is mysterious and spiritual.

Have Attitude

You see it's not the *art* form that makes worship powerful, it's the *heart* form. We could put on fantastic music productions all day, but these would contain only the art form of the external. They are the coating, the clothing—not the essence of worship. God doesn't read the externals or the posture of the body within these "art clothes." He reads our heart, not our art. God looks not as man looks. It's our attitude in the action that makes the expression worship. It is the *devotion* in the *motion* that makes the motion worship! Our best artistic productions (though well rehearsed and sincere) are just sounding brass and clanging cymbals if we have no internal heart attitude of worship.

GO VERTICAL

There will always be church leaders who want the *horizontal* focus in ministry. They will go for the "feel-goods." They will promote the preachin' machine, pump the people and hype the crowd. They will value the ear-candy and the eye-candy. They may know the difference between vertical and horizontal ministry but don't know how to change what has been modeled for them. They may mean well, but they are caught up in the earth bound system of "doing church." Perhaps they don't perceive that true worship is spiritual, honest, and transparent. They forget that Jesus looks past our best ministry presentation and looks directly at our heart.

The songs of heaven are older than humanity.

There are so many worship models available today. Leaders are clamoring to position themselves with the latest and hippest worship styles. Others simply want to go higher in true spiritual worship. If that is the case, we can't look for another man-made model and scan it over our congregation. We don't look horizontally. We must look vertically. We need to go farther up the mountain, look up, and see the perfect model—the eternal and real realm of the other side. And so here we turn to the book of the songs of aliens and elders and angels as they worship God in heaven.

The content and focus of heaven's worship is God—His character, His attributes, His acts and His pleasure. Worship is in the beauty of holiness—His otherness.

The songs of heaven are older than humanity. They are older than all of our earth models, all of the different conferences and movements that we have, and they transcend time and space. As we seek to learn about the songs from the other side, let's learn more about their rich background as described in the Revelation of Jesus Christ. This will be the focus of this book, and when you are done, I trust you will sense your own worship aligning with the worship in heaven.

SONGS AMIDST TRIALS

The apostle John wrote the book of Revelation in about AD 90 during a time when the followers of Jesus Christ were going through hard persecution in a difficult culture. This was a period of extreme adversity for believers. In AD 67, the Roman emperor, Nero, was boiling Christians in oil, nailing them to crosses and burning them alive in his garden just for the thrill of it. It is thought that during this time Peter and Paul were martyred. Christians fought discouragement and hopelessness, and John was the only surviving

SONGS FROM THE OTHER SIDE

apostle that had been with Jesus. All the rest had been killed. The book of Revelation came to John, in part to encourage the persecuted church, but it stands as a beacon of hope for all believers throughout all time.

JESUS' TEENAGE COUSIN

John was a unique individual. He was the son of Zebedee, a brother of the apostle James and a cousin to Jesus. In His early years, John ran a fishing business in Capernaum. Perhaps he worked around rowdy men who often cursed. It's possible that before he began to follow Jesus, John carried on like some sailors do. We do know that James and John were called the "sons of thunder" probably because they had loud, active personalities.

John saw Jesus as a father figure

John was one of the twelve disciples, and yet one of the three who was closest to Jesus. Some scholars say that John could have been a teenager when Jesus called him to be a disciple. That could be why he leaned upon the chest of Jesus at the Last Supper because he considered Jesus his mentor. It makes sense that a younger man would lean on a person who was dear to him, so perhaps John saw Jesus as a father figure. Later on, this teenager would develop in character to be the pastor of the church in Jerusalem!

John had been involved in Jesus' life in a major way. It was John and Peter who made preparations for the Last Supper. Jesus trusted John enough to ask him to care for His mother after His death. John was the first disciple to reach the tomb when the disciples heard the tomb was empty.

Historians say that some time after Jesus' resurrection, John left Jerusalem and took Jesus' mother with him to Ephesus. Timothy had been the pastor of the church in Ephesus. It is believed that one day he went outside of his house to greet a local crowd that was marching in the streets. Timothy started preaching to them, and they became so angry that they rose up and killed him. History says that John came and took the church. What an exciting congregation that must have been! The mother of Jesus was part of the congregation, and the pastor had been discipled by Jesus Himself.

Though the island imprisoned him, his spirit was caught up above the earth and he saw and heard the sights and sounds of what is on the other side.

Historical tradition says that Domitian was killing no less than forty thousand Christians at the time. He was considered an anti-Christ—a personification of Satan. Believers were pressured to give up their witness and indulge in sensuality. John, under the persecution of Domitian, was arrested and put in a boiling pot of oil. They would cast in a hook when the process was finished and pull out the skeleton, for the flesh would have fallen off it. However, when they emerged the hook to pull John out, he was unscathed. Domitian was enraged and didn't know what to do with this John, so he incarcerated him on the Isle called Patmos, a small volcanic Greek island close to Turkey.

This island became John's prison. His clothing was ragged sackcloth; probably he had no shoes and ate meager rations of bread and water. At eighty years of age, he was required to do hard manual labor, using only a simple hand tool to cut rocks out of a stone quarry. It is in this environment and under such cruel circumstances that John received the greatest revelation recorded of what it is like on the other side.

Think about it! This was the John who had been the youngest and closest follower of Jesus. He had been the pastor of the church in Jerusalem and in Ephesus. This is the disciple Jesus loved. Now he is in prison, personifying the condition of many Christians.

"I don't deserve this!" John could have said.

"After serving my mentor for sixty years this is all that I have to show for it!" we might have thought if we'd been John.

However, John was a humble servant of Christ who knew there was a price to pay for identifying with and preaching Christ crucified. John was not concerned about his own comforts but was focused on the kingdom and the King. Though the island imprisoned him, his spirit was caught up above the earth and he saw and heard the sights and sounds of what is on the other side. John was a worshiper.

The Keyhole

This book of Revelation is a disclosure of Jesus Christ and the worship of Him in the eternal realm. Jesus is the center of the book. This book gives us a glimpse, a keyhole look, into a truer and more real worship—a perfect model of how we are to worship. These early doxologies of the Apocalypse reflect the spirit of adoration that resounds around the throne. It is captured in this book like in no other. For here what is previously hidden is revealed and we go to the other side. These songs in Revelation represent the language of heaven and show us our destiny.

The Salmon Swim

There is more for you to experience as you go on your journey in worship. Perhaps you are dissatisfied with the worship status quo, or perhaps your pool of worship is becoming clouded with contaminants. Maybe you can't see your feet anymore as you stand in the worship waters. Are people dumping garbage into the worship atmosphere and calling this worship? Are you dissatisfied with the hype, big business, production and technology driven worship? Then maybe you should do what the ancients did and go farther up stream. Like a salmon, swim against the downward currents of the "pop-culture." Go beyond survival to higher waters where the streams flow pure and clean from the presence of God.

Let's ascend above the tree-line where few want to go. Let's stand on a higher place where the air is cleaner and we can see for miles and miles. *Let's go vertical and look up as we hear songs from the other side and the worship there.*

---

[1] John heard all these creatures "saying." It is important to note that scholars say that the Greek word for "speaking" is consistent with singing. One could conclude that this could be interpreted as literal singing. (The NIV uses the word "singing," while other translations use "saying" or other forms of speaking.) At any rate, this word "saying" is a present active participle indicating *perpetual* praise by this planet's creatures. Other source - *Leon Morris*, The Revelation of St. John (Grand Rapids, MI; Wm. B. Eerdmans, 1969), 100.

CHAPTER TWO

COME UP

After these things I looked, and behold, a door standing open in heaven. And the first voice which I heard was like a trumpet speaking with me, saying, "Come up here, and I will show you things which must take place after this."

Immediately I was in the Spirit; and behold, a throne set in heaven, and One sat on the throne.

And He who sat there was like a jasper and a sardius stone in appearance; and there was a rainbow around the throne, in appearance like an emerald.

Around the throne were twenty-four thrones, and on the thrones I saw twenty-four elders sitting, clothed in white robes; and they had crowns of gold on their heads.

And from the throne proceeded lightnings, thunderings, and voices. Seven lamps of fire were burning before the throne, which are the seven Spirits of God. (Rev. 4:1-5)

"Come up where I am," the Lord calls to John.

This prisoner's circumstances did not keep him from going vertical. I trust that whether you are in difficult or good circumstances, you will look up, too. As you do, consider the worship songs of heaven recorded in the fourth and fifth chapters of the book of Revelation. These songs from the other side give us a pattern for living and worshipping our Lord.

FROM PRISON TO PRAISE

At the age of eighty John was incarcerated for his faith on the Isle of Patmos. Despite his circumstance he is about to see and hear unusual things from the other side. We don't know whether John was beamed to heaven or if he had a vision. However what he experienced was real and tangible because he described it in detail. John's description gives us a clear record of what is on the other side:

> *After these things I looked, and behold, a door standing open in heaven. And the first voice which I heard was like a trumpet speaking with me, saying, "Come up here, and I will show you things which must take place after this" (Rev. 4:1).*

"After these things" references the vision and conversation John had earlier with Jesus concerning the seven churches (see Rev. 1-3). We don't know how much time had elapsed during or in between these visitations. However, the focus changes from the cities on earth (of which John was to write down and take to the seven churches of those cities) to heaven. John looks up.

"I looked," John says, into what possibly was the third heaven, and he sees the throne of God and the worship that occurs there. "And behold," or "Look! Listen!" the Bible dramatically accounts. A door was standing *open* in heaven.

An open door is an invitation. John looks into the concave of the firmament above him and he sees an open door. This open door is an invitation to come in and look inside. What he sees is so far above and beyond our temporal, natural world that it is almost indescribable.

The first sound John heard was a strong and mighty voice. It was loud and resembled a long blast of a trumpet. "Come up here," the voice said. It was an invitation to come up and visit the glory of the celestial world.

"Up," signifies ascension, rising above the natural world. When you hear the voice of the Lord or the Holy Spirit saying from the other side, "Come," it is an invitation to transcend the realm of your limited perception of reality and see the Father. It is an opportunity to go up to a place with Him that is higher than where you are now. Your body may not go anywhere, but your spirit is caught up.

> *Worshippers know what it is to invoke the presence of God in worship—in any place and at any time.*

When you come into the presence of God and get close to the Source of life, you go up. When you lead people in worship and encourage them to come into His presence with singing, you help them ascend.

John's negative circumstances did not keep him from going vertical. I trust when we are elderly and locked up in prison, having nothing on our feet, wearing scratchy bags for clothing and surviving on only bread and water, that we would worship! When and whether we worship has nothing to do with our circumstances because worshippers know what it is to invoke the presence of God in worship—in any place and at any time.

"Come up where I am," says the Lord. The place where the voice came from was higher than where John was. And the exciting thing is that God invited John to come to where He was. The invitation of the Lord is the same to us today in the midst of clergy sex scandals, corporate corruption, layoffs, missing children and men at war: *Arise, climb up, ascend, come up to a higher place—the place of God's presence.*

After the voice invited John to come up, what happened next? The voice promised to show John things that must take place after this. Here God promised to reveal the unknown, to reveal what will happen in the future. His purpose is not to provide a timetable to pinpoint exactly when these things will be. His point is to focus us on the heavenly realm.

BEAMED UP

Immediately I was in the Spirit; and behold, a throne set in heaven, and One sat on the throne (Rev. 4:2).

"At once, I was absorbed, caught up, overwhelmed; I went to another dimension," John said. He was caught up in a spiritual trance and saw the visions of God. Suddenly, somehow, he found himself present in the third heaven. We know that this experience was real because John had all of his senses—his ears heard, his eyes saw, his mouth spoke, and his heart had the capacity to weep.

There we will stand with all of the redeemed and the angels and sing the songs of the other side while playing the harps of God

"And behold, a throne *set* in heaven" (italics added). In other words, the throne was fastened, fixed, permanent, and ordered. The first thing that John sees when he looks through the heavenly porthole is a throne and its occupant. The whole universe, all of eternal dimension and everything beyond the tangible and the temporal, are centered on the throne. God's throne is the center of all things.

In John's culture, the throne of Caesar was the center of all authority in the earthly Roman world. Yet John saw another throne established high above the Roman Empire and far above the earth.

Only one sat on the throne, not a committee. It wasn't a democracy, for in the kingdom of God people have no voice or vote. We submitted them to God when we gave our lives to Christ and found a higher destiny as a result.

Contrary to our idealized notions, our destiny is not to live in heaven to play golf or flit around the clouds with little harps. Our destiny is to come before the throne and endlessly worship Him. We will sing for millenniums and never have to clear our throats, get a drink of water or have a Sunday afternoon nap. For we will have shed our worn-out "earth suit" and put on a celestial "spirit suit" that will never fade.

Our work as priests unto God is the destiny of all of us who believe in Christ. It's our eternal act of worship. There we will stand with all of the redeemed and the angels and sing the songs of the other side while playing the harps of God.

GOD'S APPEARANCE

And He who sat there was like a jasper and a sardius stone in appearance; and there was a rainbow around the throne, in appearance like an emerald (Rev. 4:3).

Imagine how hard it must have been for John to describe the splendor of what he experienced because he'd never seen anything like it before! That is why he uses the literary device of comparison instead of actual description. This form of communication is used often by those who have seen the other side for the simple reason that there is nothing on this side exactly like what is in the other.

John writes that God looked like the precious stones of jasper and sardius. Jasper is opaque red and yellow-like quartz. It was the last stone in the high priest's breastplate (Ex. 28:20) and speaks of the dazzling brightness of God's presence. Sardius was the first stone in the high priest's breastplate (Ex. 28:17) and very possibly was blood red. When Scripture says the seated King had the appearance of diamond-like jasper and ruby red sardius, it speaks of God's glory and His purity on one hand and His justice and redemption on the other. The impression is that God is extremely pure and very holy or altogether other than anything around Him or anything else that exists. He stands alone brilliant in purity and splendor, perfect in justice and salvation.

> *Loud voices and thunderclaps let all know of the power of the One on the throne.*

GREEN HALO

John went on to describe what was around the throne: a rainbow that looked like an emerald. This bright green halo is reminiscent of God's covenant with His people after the flood. The rainbow is a symbol of living hope in the midst of judgment, the assurance of grace and God's faithfulness to keep His promises. Above the lightning, the thunder and the voices that are coming from the throne, John sees a rainbow assuring all there is mercy.

There is peace around the throne even though there is such potentially violent power in the midst of the throne. God's power is potent and is of potential danger to His creation. God is big, great, and all-powerful. He is out of our control, and so we feel godly fear and awe in His mighty presence. Loud voices and thunderclaps let all know of the power of the One on the throne. Yet the rainbow of mercy assures all of us who come near that He won't ultimately hurt us.

THE EARTHLINGS

*Around the throne were twenty-four thrones, and on the thrones
I saw twenty-four elders sitting, clothed in white robes; and they had
crowns of gold on their heads (Rev. 4:4).*

This scene depicts one of the connections between the human race on earth and worship in heaven. Circling God's central throne were twenty-four lesser thrones on which twenty-four elders, or rulers, sat. These elders are not angels or aliens. They are men from earth's realm who represent kings and priests.

We know that these human rulers have regal notoriety because they are sitting on thrones and have gold crowns. A throne is a seat of power and authority, a place where a monarch sits when he executes judgments, passes sentences and makes decrees.

Among the Jews, the elders were a council of judges (or counselors) who would rule and represent God, making decisions and giving wisdom to the people. Some scholars say the twenty-four elders described in Revelation represent the twelve tribes of Israel in the Old Testament and the twelve apostles in the New Testament. These elders in heaven denote aged and venerable men of wisdom. They don't necessarily hold a "church office" as we perceive it; their role is to sit, rule and judge as a counselor or justice.

We know these elders are priests because there are twenty-four of them. They are probably the heavenly counterparts to the twenty-four groups of temple priests who ministered continuously before the Ark of the Covenant (see 1 Chron. 24:1-31). The mercy seat on the top of the ark is referred to as the throne of God. Above the mercy throne was a real-in-the-earth tangible expression of the presence of God. It was called the "*shekinah*" presence. Today, the whole church is a company of priests who render perpetual praise and glory to the Almighty in His presence.

> *The* **whole church** *is a company of* **priests** *who render perpetual* **praise** *and* **glory** *to the* **Almighty** *in* **His presence.**

These priestly kings are clothed in white indicating their righteousness and purity. It's interesting to note that priestly garments in the Old Testament were made of fine linen (see Exodus 28:5-8). The finest linen was expensive in this culture. Rich and powerful kings, queens and their royal courts, as well as the priests, wore fine linen. Linen allowed free circulation of air and kept the wearer cool in hot climates. The application here is this: we are not to sweat in the presence of God or wear anything that causes us to sweat when we worship Him. In worship, we do not need to work it up, hype or pump the crowd. If we bring people to an awareness of God, they will worship.

> *The elements of nature convulse around the throne because of the power of the One who sits there.*

These priestly kings in heaven also had crowns of gold. Crowns were symbols of ultimate triumph and many times were given to victors in war or competitive sports. Here the crowns represent victorious faith in God—not merely political authority.

THRONE STORMS

And from the throne proceeded lightnings, thunderings, and voices. Seven lamps of fire were burning before the throne, which are the seven Spirits of God (Rev. 4:5).

The presence of God is a dangerous and noisy place. His presence is dangerous because it has a force that no earthling can stand. The Bible says, "For our God is a consuming fire" (Heb. 12:29).

We tend to process Scripture through earth filters. When we think of the fire of God's presence, we may think in terms of a controlled fire—a warm fireplace glow or a Bic™ lighter flame. That's not our God! He's dangerous because He is out of *our* control. He can come in and burn stuff up— we could look like a burnt matchstick if He comes near in His majesty and power! He is consuming fire.

When we pray and sing, "Send the fire, Lord," do we really mean that? Do we want that kind of fire? Do we want the whole landscape changed or do we just want the warm glow of a "feel-good" moment?

When it hailed inside that building in Mexico where worship was ascending to heaven, it indicated the extent of the power of God's presence.

God is dangerous, and His awesome glory is likened to continuous thunder and lightning. There are thunderstorms in and around His throne that never stop. Lightning plays around the throne, clapping thunderously to announce the presence of an all-powerful God. The power of His presence is stronger than a nuclear bomb. It surpasses the intensity of the fireball we call the sun. God's powerful presence goes far beyond anything we have ever experienced. The elements of nature convulse around the throne because of the power of the One who sits there.

A friend told me of a small church in central Mexico that was experiencing signs and wonders during worship. The people met in a storefront on a dusty main street of their small town. It took over three hours to get there by bus from the nearest airport. People came because they wanted to worship the Lord.

The musicians were not extremely talented but were very hungry to get closer to God. Therefore they would worship most of the day. In one of the meetings it was reported that hail began to fall inside the building during worship. There were no storms outside to generate the hail, only *the storm of the power of God's presence.*

Hail storms in Texas where I live can be very powerful. The rain freezes before it can fall to the earth and is thrown back up into the air and another layer freezes around the first. This is repeated constantly. The size of hail is determined by the violence of the storm, and some hailstones when they reach the ground are as big as grapefruit. Stones this large can break a person's arm or leave cars and buildings with extreme damage. Hail is an indication of violent turbulence above the earth.

When it hailed inside that building in Mexico where worship was ascending to heaven, it indicated the extent of the power of God's presence. Some of the people in the service experienced the

Lord's power so strongly that it felt like they were experiencing earthquakes. The Lord was shaking not only their priorities and their preconceived ideas, but their bodies as well. Shaking and quaking is often connected with God's presence. Isaiah saw door jams shake when the presence of God filled the temple (Isaiah 6:4).

The picture of what John saw and heard on the other side was tumultuous and violent. The elements of nature convulsed around the throne because of the One who sat there.

THE ILLUMINATOR

In front of the throne, seven lamps of spirit fire were blazing. "Seven" appears often in the book of Revelation. (For example, there were the seven churches, the seven candlesticks, the seven angels, the seven spirits, the seven seals, the seven trumpets, the seven vials, the seven stars, the seven horns, the seven eyes, the seven lamps, the seven thunders, the seven headed dragon with seven crowns, the seven mountains, and the seven kings.) "Seven" speaks of completeness, totality, fullness and perfection and represents an awesome picture of perfect completeness in heaven.

These seven lamps of fire are the seven Spirits of God, the Holy Spirit. This scene in heaven represents the perfect work of the Holy Spirit as He illumines and purifies.

A CALL FROM THE WILD

"Come up here," God said to John. John obeyed, and heaven opened to him, giving him a glimpse of marvelous and glorious things. The word to us is to come up to where we can see God. You don't have to stay down. Arise, ascend, arise to your rest, and transcend the trouble, trial and terror. Pray with Rev. Johnson Oatman when he sang over 100 years ago:

> I want to scale the utmost height,
> And catch a gleam of glory bright;
> But still I'll pray till heav'n I've found,
> "Lord, lead me on to higher ground."

> Lord, lift me up and let me stand,
> By faith on heaven's tableland,
> A higher plane than I have found;
> Lord, plant my feet on higher ground[1].

---

[1] Johnson Oatman, Jr., "Higher Ground," © 1926 Renewal Public Domain.

CHAPTER THREE

THE ALIEN ANTHEM

Before the throne there was a sea of glass, like crystal. And in the midst of the throne, and around the throne, were four living creatures full of eyes in front and in back.

The first living creature was like a lion, the second living creature like a calf, the third living creature had a face like a man, and the fourth living creature was like a flying eagle.

The four living creatures, each having six wings, were full of eyes around and within. And they do not rest day or night, saying:

"Holy, holy, holy, Lord God Almighty,
Who was and is and is to come!" (Revelation 4:6-8)

John saw an open door in the heavens, and through this portal God invited him to look into the glory of other side. The obedient servant recorded what he experienced—majestic songs and brilliant visions that surpassed anything he had ever seen or heard. As we, too, accept God's invitation to worship Him, we gain a heavenly perspective through His holy Word. We hear songs from the other side. These songs humble us and transform us. They give us a pattern for worship that is real and spiritual.

If we have a higher view of God, we can have higher worship. The greater we depict God, the more we lift Him up and declare His attributes, the more people will *want* to worship Him.

When I contemplate Him and His greatness and grandeur, I begin to explode with perpetual praise and extemporaneous exultation. My prayer is that you are sensing that same thing right now as you read this book. I am, as I am writing.

We now look to extra-celestial beings and the song they sing in heaven. The scene is God's throne and the sea in front of it.

THE CRYSTALLINE SEA

Before the throne there was a sea of glass, like crystal (Rev. 6a).

A pellucid pavement, shimmering like crystal, spreads out as an ocean before God's royal throne. Imagine what the sea of glass looks like—a wide space that mirrors the splendid multi-colored lights emanating from the throne. The vast expanse of this crystalline sea cushions the presence of God who dwells in unapproachable light, utterly transcendent and separate from all that He has made. I believe this sea is an emblem of calmness, peace and majesty.

THE ALIENS

And in the midst of the throne, and around the throne,
were four living creatures full of eyes in front and in back (Rev. 4:6b).

These four celestial creatures stood in and around the throne making an inner circle. Some think they were possibly supporting the throne. However they were definitely in the middle of the action and very conspicuous.

The living creatures were unlike anything John had ever seen. Some translators use the term "beasts," not to be confused with the vicious beast found with the false prophet and the anti-Christ later in Revelation. They were not human, animal or angel. I prefer to call these creatures aliens, because the word "alien" means belonging to another place or from a foreign land. From their description, they certainly are not from around here! Suffice it to say they were intelligent extra-celestial beings.

Very possibly these were cherubs like the ones guarding the Garden of Eden. It is thought that these were the creatures depicted on the veil of the tabernacle, on the Ark of the Covenant, and in the temple of Solomon. They were winged cherubic beings often associated with the worship and the presence of God. Often, Scripture talks about God dwelling between the cherubim or enthroned upon the cherubim. They were connected with the revealed presence of God.

These celestial entities are guardians of the throne. They live in the immediate presence of God continually and proclaim God's glory. I believe that they initiate and lead worship on the other side.

There were four living creatures. "Four" speaks of the four points of the compass, representing the whole created cosmos. This fourfold description here emphasizes the universality of this creaturely worship. All worshippers are to worship Him and live in His presence constantly. These aliens represent the supreme government of God over the four "corners" of the earth and beyond.

They were winged cherubic beings often associated with the worship and the presence of God.

One of the great mysteries about the celestial beings is that they are covered with eyes in front and back. They are the seers and the throne attendants, always looking toward the throne and able to see in all directions. It could be said that these creatures depict the all-seeing posture leaders are to have, which is to watch and wait upon God, surveying His creation. They always perceive with an eye constantly on the enthroned One as they watch and guard the throne. Likewise leaders of worship should always be watching the throne and attending to Yahweh, our sovereign Potentate and gracious Savior.

THE CELESTIAL QUARTET

The first living creature was like a lion, the second living creature like a calf, the third living creature had a face like a man, and the fourth living creature was like a flying eagle (Rev. 4:7).

These aliens were unlike anything John had ever seen. He had nothing to compare them to except those animals with which he was familiar.

The first creature was said to be like a lion. Lions speak of nobility, monarchy, royalty and authority. They could represent the kings that we are to be unto God. You see we are kings (and priests) to *God*, not to *people*. We can't build our empires of our own following; we are holy servants of the Most High.

The second living creature was like a calf or a young ox. In an agricultural society, these animals bore the heavy workloads. You could say they were the "farm tractors" of the Old Testament. The calf speaks to us of the work, strength, sacrifice and the servant-hood of being one of God's leaders.

The next extra-celestial had the face like a man, which speaks of wisdom and intelligence. Man was the king of God's creation who was commissioned to take dominion over all that was made. The fact that this alien's face looked human connects the creature (and the activity of heaven) to the realm of those people who dwell on earth.

The fourth living creature was like a flying eagle, which speaks of ascension and swiftness. Note this eagle is not perched, but is flying.

The soaring eagle speaks to me of prayer and praise. The Hebrew word that the Old Testament uses for prayer is *tephillah*; for praise *tehillah*. These words are one letter apart; both are musical terms—songs of prayer and songs of praise. They are two portholes into the presence of God, two entrances to the other side, two ways to go vertical. These twin-wings of prayer and praise help us ascend to great heights in God's presence.

> *The fact that this* **alien's face** looked *human connects the* **creature** *to the* **realm** *of those people who dwell on earth.*

EAGLES OR CHICKENS

It is interesting that the Bible tells us to mount up with wings like eagles (Is. 40:31), and not like chickens! Have you ever seen worship leaders lead like chickens? Chickens work so hard to fly, but they don't get very high. With feathers and dust flying everywhere, there is effort, commotion, and screaming, "I can't hear you!" But the sad outcome is that chickens remain on the ground in their "coops," tired and unchanged, gaining no altitude. They don't know that God has unlocked the door with the key of David. At any time they can get out of the coop and soar in the heavens because Christians who become worshipers become eagles. They have an appetite for altitude and not pecking on earth. They don't know that there's a better place, there is a better experience, a higher realm of worship and living.

How much better it is to teach people how to soar like eagles in worship! Eagles effortlessly transcend barriers to flight. They flap just a little bit as they ride the up-currents of the wind God sends. Eagles know how to soar and how to ascend to greater heights.

These dragonfly-like creatures hover above God's throne like huge helicopters.

You are made for ascension. You have an appetite for altitude and the presence of God because your DNA is not that of a chicken but an eagle.

The Christian fathers believed there was an association between these four creatures and the four Gospels. The lion represented the gospel of Matthew that reveals Christ as King. The ox referenced what Mark talked about when describing the laborious endurance of Jesus. Doctor Luke wrote about the human sympathy that Jesus had for mankind. The eagle is reminiscent of what John revealed in his gospel about the transcendent majesty of the Word made flesh.

EYES AND HELICOPTERS

The four living creatures, each having six wings, were full of eyes around and within. And they do not rest day or night (Rev. 4:8a).

These extra-celestials were much like the seraphim that Isaiah saw in the temple when he was worshiping. "Each one had six wings: with two he covered his face, with two he covered his feet, and with two he flew" (Is. 6:2). Isaiah saw these dragonfly-like creatures hover above God's throne like huge helicopters. When commissioned, they race to do the royal bidding of the enthroned One, all the while keeping their face and feet covered. This probably indicates they are not to be seen and that they only go where God sends them. Similar to the beings in Revelation, Isaiah 6:3 says these seraphim cry out, "Holy is the Lord."

One of the great mysteries about the aliens described in Revelation is that they were full of eyes as mentioned earlier in verse six. Only this time the Scripture adds that these eyes were all around and inside. One scholar has suggested that they had eyes under their wings. We do not know for sure. But the eyes were inside and out indicating perfect insight within and without.

"They do not rest day or night." Unlike organic humans, these extra-celestials do not need to sleep, eat or rejuvenate in any way. Their worship is totally zealous, and it never ceases. Continuously and unbroken, their voices rise to exalt the Lord. Their worship reoccurs seamlessly and incessantly. It is non-stop, 24/7. The picture here is of perpetual praise, endless eulogy and ceaseless citation. This is the life of those who live closest to the presence of God—a continuous and eternal exultation of the goodness of God.

Does this sound like the worship of your church? I'm not talking about your church meeting or the program that you planned. I'm talking about the church, the family of believers, the temples of worship that walk through life in their earth suits. Isn't this what the temples of the Holy Spirit are to do—worship?

ALIENS SING

As John peers into heaven through heaven's open door, he *sees* the reverent and profound worship of the inhabitants, and he *hears* the sound of worship on the other side. He hears these lyrics:

> *"Holy, holy, holy*
> *Lord God Almighty,*
> *Who was and is and is to come!" (Rev. 4:8b)*

This is the first song of some twenty-eight songs from the other side listed in the Apocalypse. The lyrics the aliens sing are about Yahweh and His nature. It starts with a three-fold affirmation, "Holy, holy, holy," which speaks of the Trinity of the persons of the Godhead, equally divine in their attributes. Holy is the Father, holy is the Son and holy is the Holy Spirit, three in one. He is holy who was and is and will be. The creatures are so captured by whom God is that they never stop, never grow tired of saying this one word, "holy."

Some people say, "Well, we sang this song twice, so do we have to sing it again?" It isn't for *you*, it is for God. Heaven's creatures endlessly declare His greatness, His grandeur, His mystery and His majesty—for He is all that and much more—so why shouldn't we? Why would we stop praising Him? Is it possible to come to an end of the acclamations, declarations and proclamations of who He is?

Heaven's creatures endlessly declare His greatness, His grandeur, His mystery and His majesty.

God is eternal, continuous, all encompassing, the same yesterday, today and forever, so why would we ever cease to praise Him? He is deserving of continual worship.

Holiness is the quality most basic to the essential nature of God. Scholars say it's His crowning attribute. His holiness sums up all His other attributes—His infinitude, His immutableness, His omniscience, His omnipresence and the rest. The root word of "holy" means "separate" or "apart," indicating God's self-existence and independence from everything He created. He doesn't need us, or anything from us.

You could say that the "hot worship" of heaven that comes from these extra-celestials begins with their acknowledgement of God's holiness. Their transcendent lyrics of the attributes and nature of God are simple, but staggering. The initial song here in the Apocalypse declares God's design for all of His creatures from the four corners of the earth: All living creatures are to lift up His crowning attribute—His holiness.

CANNONS & FIREWORKS

The aliens also say the words, "Lord God Almighty," speaking of His all-powerfulness and His lordship over all things. Jeremiah tells us that He made the heavens and the earth by His "great power and outstretched arm," and "nothing is too hard" for Him (32:17). With just a word, He can strike every creature to the ground. "There is no God besides Me; I kill and I make alive; I wound and I heal; nor is there any who can deliver from My hand" (Deut. 32:39). That's the power of the God we serve.

There's an interesting story told of Louis XIV's funeral. After the priest looked down at the casket containing the body of the once-powerful monarch of France with luxurious robes of royalty concealing the cold form within, he turned to the assembled nobility present and began his oration: "My friends, only God is great."

We must remind ourselves and remind each other, great is the Lord and greatly to be praised. A little whimper won't do it. A little cry, "Jesus," isn't enough. We must declare with a volume of thunder and lightning, with cannons and fireworks, with trumpets and crashing cymbals how great and grandiose our God is. He indeed is all-powerful—the Lord God the Almighty. We are to praise Him according to His excellent greatness.

Then the aliens sing, "Who was and is and is to come!" Completing the trilogy is the reference to His infinitude. The God who is *holy* and *omnipotent* is also *eternal.* In this song the number three is compounded by the succession of the three phrases each with three descriptions of God. Three times holy—holy who was, holy who is and holy who is to come. God is forever the same. His nature will not change; He is from everlasting to everlasting. This quality of God causes ceaseless praise among the hosts of heaven. So why don't we worship Him like this, as spirit-beings who have been redeemed by the blood of Jesus? Why not come into God's timeless presence and know Him in greater measure.

> The *God* we serve *stands* above time, and He is *free* from all earthly *distinctions*. He has no *creation* and no succession.

FLYING LOW

This worship song in heaven immediately brings one to contemplate the essence of the divine nature because His being is the foundation of all His deeds. So before telling us what God *does*, the heavenly creatures tell us *who* He is. Before we put Him to work and say, "He's *my* healer, He's *my* deliverer, He's *my* Savior," we should declare His personality and character.

It is okay to sing about what God has done for us from time to time. But generally there is too much of "me" and "my" in the songs we sing to God. If that is all we sing about, our worship is too low and we are flying at a low altitude. When we lower God to our level and keep Him horizontal, we make Him little more than rabbit's foot in our pocket, or a masseuse who helps us feel better. There is no compelling

Before telling us what God does, the heavenly creatures tell us who He is.

reason for people to worship Him! Then let's focus on Him first and all of His greatness, grandeur, power and majesty.

IN THE ZONE

A recent poll found that nearly one third of all Christians have never experienced the presence of God at any time in their lives or in any public worship service. Many believers don't know what it is to ascend into the presence of God and let the greatness of God overwhelm them. Many people have never experienced the presence of God to the extent that they begin to weep and fall to their faces because He is so awesome.

The God we serve stands above time, and He is free from all earthly distinctions. He has no creation and no succession. He has no beginning, and He will never end. Our loving God is absolutely holy.

God is His own existence. He is His own reason and He is His own cause.

The theme of God's sovereignty is missing in many of our songs and sermons. We like to think that we are self-sufficient and God's little helpers. There are a few songwriters who write transcendent lyrics. It's evident that they are worshipers because they have been "in the zone." They have seen through heaven's door something higher than them. When you choose songs for a worship service, pick those kinds of songs. Reveal God more than you have before in your conversation, prayer and worship.

It is a blow to human pride to acknowledge that the Almighty needs nothing from us to complete His perfection in witness or worship. But even the scenes of heaven's joyful worship are not for His benefit as if He lacked something in Himself. God is

His own existence. He is His own reason and He is His own cause. His is His own activity and He is above every compulsion, every desire and every fate. He is above all and beyond all. This alien song depicts total submission to the King who sits on the throne.

A COMPELLING PICTURE

Leaders wonder why congregates don't enter into worship. Perhaps this is because we don't present a compelling picture of what He is really like. To lead people in worship, we need to be students of theology more than students of music. Poetic musical compositions in themselves don't compel people to worship God. But the more we know about God, His holiness, His greatness, and His eternalness, the more we can accurately depict Him in our lyrics, prayers or preaching. Our description of God will invite people to go up, to ascend, to be sucked into the vacuum of high "outer-space" worship like it is on the other side.

Why not let the Spirit draw you up. Get out of the way and let the greatness of God overwhelm you. Go up, and take some worshippers with you. Let us cry out with the living creatures:

"Holy, holy, holy,
Lord God Almighty,
Who was and is and is to come

CHAPTER FOUR

HEAVEN'S WORSHIP LEADERS

Whenever the living creatures give glory and honor and thanks to Him who sits on the throne, who lives forever and ever,

The twenty-four elders fall down before Him who sits on the throne and worship Him who lives forever and ever, and cast their crowns before the throne. (Rev. 4:9, 10)

Inside each of us is a yearning to get in the "throne zone." It's almost like there is a vacuum inside that desires to be filled with presence of God. We feel drawn to get into the place for which we were created. This is because God *created* us to be worshippers in His presence.

Our goal as worship leaders and pastors is to lead people up into the transcendent presence of God. It is to initiate worship that brings people to that place they were created to be with Him. The living creatures in the book of Revelation have this same role, and I am absolutely amazed by what they do. These celestial worship leaders demonstrate how to lead awe-inspiring worship of our living Lord.

CELESTIAL INITIATORS

As we look to the other side, we have seen the throne of God surrounded by twenty-four elders and by four living creatures that worship Him who sits on the throne. Now the focus is on the action of the living creatures and what they do:

> *Whenever the living creatures give glory and honor and thanks to Him who sits on the throne, who lives forever and ever, the twenty-four elders fall down before Him who sits on the throne and worship (Rev. 4:9, 10a).*

These living aliens appear to be initiators of worship because others respond to their action and adoration of God. At their initiation, the twenty-four elders worship with extreme expression.

Note that the Scripture says *whenever* the living creatures give glory to God, something else happens. This word "whenever" suggests that each and every time the aliens worship before the throne, the elders respond. It doesn't speak of *at one time*; it could be *anytime* or *anywhere*.

TERRESTRIAL INITIATORS

As leaders of worship we don't make, create or manufacture worship. We don't plan or produce worship. We just simply initiate worship.

Some church organizations have worship planners. Do those words ("worship" and "planning") really go together? The idea of worship planning takes worship out of the organic realm of earthlings who try to ascend spiritually and relationally and makes it systematic. To look at it another way, if you wanted to spend time with your spouse, wouldn't it be awkward to use the term "romantic planning"? The phrase "worship planner" puts worship on a pre-planned, practiced and produced level of the organized. This takes us down the path of producing programs or systems and calling it worship, and perhaps never knowing the presence of God. Sure, there is a need to prepare songs and messages but let's not remove the mysterious and (prophetic) spiritual qualities of worship.

*These **living** aliens appear to be **initiators** of **worship** because others respond to their **action** and **adoration** of God.*

There is a place for planning and organizing when it comes to ministry to people. But worship is on another level. It is "heart to heart," not "head to head." When we want to look good and to impress people—that is the same attitude Lucifer had. (Ouch!) He was perfect in beauty, and he thought he would ascend into the heights of heaven. "I will be like the Most High," he thought, "I will exalt my throne above the stars of God" (See Is. 14:13, 14.) He was only concerned about image. The tendency to slip into that attitude of pride is in all of us. Don't do it!

THE COOK AND THE RECIPE

In contrast, the four living creatures bestow accolades to God. They sing, "Glory and honor and thanks to Him."

Glory is a visible manifestation of the splendor of God's divine attributes. "Glory" also can mean "praise"—audible honorable praise of God's subjects to this great Sovereign who sits on His emerald throne.

The word "honor" means to give value and esteem in the highest possible degree. When we consider someone to be precious and priceless, we esteem him. So with the One on the throne, we render priceless value and give Him dignity.

The heavenly creatures also say thanks to God and give Him gratitude. These creatures, as well as *all* creatures, should *always* be grateful to the One who created them.

There are two reasons why we are to worship God: because we exist and because we are saved. Our Creator created us, and we need to worship our manufacturer and thank him with gratitude for being alive. Our Savior redeemed us, and we need to worship God because Jesus died on the Cross for our sins and rose again. So, we sing gratefully because He purchased our salvation and because we exist.

God can jump into the middle of the recipe and manifest Himself among the ingredients and then jump out again because He lives above it.

After singing "glory" and "honor" and "thanks" to Him who sits on the throne, the four living creatures say, "Who lives forever and ever." They reveal something of God's life. He lives, but He just doesn't live, He lives and lives, and lives some more! Oh yes, once He died, but He rose again, and He lives and He lives and He keeps on living because He not only possesses life, He *is* life. He is not part of the creation that He made. He is above and beyond it and is not subject to its laws and forces. He is life and therefore continues living. He is like the cook that made the recipe. He can change it any way He wants. God can jump into the middle of the recipe and manifest Himself among the ingredients and then jump out again because He lives above it.

FOUR FACES—ONE HEAD

The four extra-celestial creatures described by John are very unique and beautiful in their capacity to inspire worship. Ezekiel also had a vision of four living creatures, and it's a fascinating study to compare the two (Rev. 4:7; Ezek. 1:1-28). Both had likenesses of a man, lion, calf and an eagle.

Ezekiel starts his book describing a vision of God where, like John, "the heavens were opened" (Ezek. 1:1). He goes on to say he saw the four living creatures (1:5). They had bodies that reminded him of men, with likenesses of legs, feet, hands and faces. Ezekiel says each creature had four faces (v.6), and "each had the face of a man; each of the four had the face of a lion on the right side, each of the four had the face of an ox on the left side, and each of the four had the face of an eagle" (v. 10).

One could assume that since the lion and the oxen faces are on either side, and because the eagle face is mentioned last, that the eagle is in the back. You remember from our earlier study that the eagle references ascension, prayer and praise (*tephillah* and *tehillah* in the Hebrew are translated "pray" and "praise"). If this is true about the position of the eagle face, it could be said that prayer and praise has you covered; it has your back.

Verse seven says that these creatures had feet and legs that did not turn or bend. There were probably no knees in these legs. (This is a creature you have *never* seen at the zoo!) This tells us that they had no desire of moving away from God's presence, direction or mission. They would not do anything other than what the One on the throne said. They are single-minded and straightforward. They never bend or turn away to another's will.

The verse continues to say their feet were like the soles of calves' feet. I lived on a farm when I was very young. We had mostly pigs and chickens but a few cows. Instead of a single hoof or flap, cows have split hooves that enhance their maneuverability. This kind of hoof on each of the four creatures represents flexibility and agility. In addition, their feet and legs sparkled brightly like burnished bronze. These must have been brilliant, beautiful creatures.

The extra-celestials had wings with what looked like human hands underneath the wings (v. 8). Two stretched out and two stretched down to cover their bodies as if they didn't want to be seen. What goes on in the other side is not about them, but about God. Sometimes all four wings covered their bodies (v. 23).

The sound of their wings when they moved was like a mighty waterfall or the sound of a charging army. It resembled the voice of the all-powerful one, Yahweh the Almighty (v. 24). They were four, yet connected and combined as one creature. Sometimes their wings joined, which speaks of unity. They were of one purpose.

GYROSCOPES, FIRE CLOUDS AND CRYSTAL ICE

The aliens in Ezekiel had wheels and rims around them. Each alien had an identical wheel on the ground beside it. There was another wheel inside that wheel. This was a gyroscope in effect, and the spirit and life of the beings were in the wheel rims. The rims were filled with eyes, and they were so high it must have been an awe-inspiring sight. (See Ezek. 1:15-21.)

The gyroscopes, these wheels within a wheel, speak of fluid mobility. The creatures were absolutely awesome in the way they moved. They were able and willing to go any direction without ever moving or turning left or right.

These celestial aliens looked like they were inside a giant fire cloud that glowed like melting gold and flashed with dazzling brightness.

I believe that leaders, whether parents, pastors, managers or worship leaders, can learn from the qualities of these living creatures. Like them, leaders are to be seers, to have vision and have eyes for every situation. We are to look in all directions and have complete perspective. We need to be intuitive and have prophetic perspective.

These creatures had wings stretched upward and outward toward the heavens in a praise posture. When we worship, it is important to cover ourselves, making ourselves virtually "invisible" because worship is not about us. We don't need to be center stage; rather we point the way to Jesus. We need to get out of the way so people can connect with God. Leaders are facilitators. They do not bend or move from their direction and they don't turn from before the throne, though they can move in any direction.

These celestial aliens looked like they were inside a giant fire cloud that glowed like melting gold and flashed with dazzling brightness. Moving in between them were "torches" of bright fire. Out of the fire came lightning bolts (v. 13). Remember that the fire of God is not a man-controlled fire. We say, "Oh, Jesus, you make me feel so good." We need to realize that God is out of our control. He is all-powerful, more powerful than we can stand. He loves us, yet there is a side to Him that inspires a holy reverence. If God did not veil His power to us, it could destroy us. We need to trust Him in His power.

The sky over the heads of the creatures shone with awesome crystal ice. A glittering sapphire-colored throne on which the sovereign One sat was above them (vv. 22, 26). That's the example of leadership by these alien creatures who live in the power zone of the throne of God. And that is our goal as spiritual leaders as well—to live in the brilliant power zone of God. We don't move away from His presence; we stay under His leadership.

OPULENT OBEISANCE

Moving our focus back to Revelation, we saw that, just like the creatures in Ezekiel, the four living creatures around God's throne exist to worship Him. John writes that each time the living creatures give God glory, honor and thanks, the following happens:

The twenty-four elders fall down before Him who sits on the throne and worship Him who lives forever and ever, and cast their crowns before the throne (Rev 4:10).

These elders (some scholars use the term "heavenly council of counselors") were first described in verse four of this chapter. We noted that the elders have distinct thrones, glorious yet lower than

God's throne. We also noted that these leaders are a prototype of twenty-four courses of priests that serve in the temple continuously with cymbals and harps. These men represent double the number of twelve associated with divine government. Twelve speaks of perfect government, so these could represent a magnified government. They are governmental leaders, not only in man's government but they are spiritual rulers and leaders.

Whenever the living creatures initiate worship, the elders get off their thrones and fall down in total obeisance before the sovereign One. This models for all of us in leadership, whether we are parents, politicians, CEOs, pastors or apostles that we are to fall at the feet of God, our sovereign ruler in opulent obeisance.

Note that verse ten distinctly says that they *worship* Him. Often worship means to prostrate oneself in homage, but there is a distinction here. They worshiped or prostrated *and* they fell down. They honored and revered God by prostration and again with homage.

In verse nine the descriptive term for God "who lives forever and ever" is mentioned and then repeated in verse ten. This is an emphasis of the life power of God. There is a revelation of life among them.

In the midst of all of this, the elders cast their crowns down. The word "crown" here means "to twine or weave." These crowns were chaplets or badges of royalty, symbols of honor like a prize in public games. They were like victory garlands that the Romans would use or wear when they returned victorious in battle. They were trophies and symbolized things they conquered or achieved.

They take their ***trophies*** *and* ***achievements*** *and violently cast them toward Him and fall in total* ***submission.***

All of our trophies, all of our prizes, all of our accomplishments, all of our endorsements, all of our titles, all of our positions are to be laid at the feet of the Sovereign King on the throne. Even our spiritual "victories" are to be released. All reminders of what we have done are laid aside.

Scholars suggest that the elders threw their crowns violently before the throne. This could imply that they are at a distance because of His dazzling holiness. At any rate, they take their trophies and achievements and violently cast them toward Him and fall in total submission. This doesn't only occur once or twice, but it continues endlessly in heaven.

The fact that the crowns were of gold speaks of the divine nature the elders received from Christ. These men know that every good thing they have graciously received comes to them not of their own merit but as a gift of the generosity of God. In recognition of His worthiness and total submission to Him, they remove their trophies and cast them before He who gave them to them.

Likewise, may we walk humbly before our Heavenly Father. We don't need to impress others with our achievements, pictures or fashions. We don't need to pitch and promote ourselves to those we lead. Again, it is not about us. We are to promote Him. To do that we dress accordingly, act appropriately and play our music in a manner that draws people away from us and to the throne.

HOLY, HOLY, HOLY

Who among us hasn't sung this great hymn of adoration and praise? Based on these passages from Revelation and written more than 150 years ago, its timeless message inspires us today. This is because worship around the throne never ceases, and we hear its heavenly strains from the other side.

Why not join in:

Holy, holy, holy!

All the saints adore Thee,

Casting down their golden crowns around the glassy sea;

Cherubim and seraphim falling down before Thee,

Which wert, and art, and evermore shalt be.

Holy, holy, holy!

Lord God Almighty!

All Thy works shall praise Thy Name,

   in earth, and sky, and sea;

Holy, holy, holy, merciful and mighty!

God in Three Persons, blessed Trinity![1]

---

[1] Reginald Heber, "Holy, Holy, Holy," 1783-1826, NICAEA Public Domain.

CHAPTER FIVE

THE CREATION CANTICLE

"You are worthy, O Lord,
To receive glory and honor and power;
For You created all things,
And by Your will they exist and were created."
(Rev. 4:11)

Think about this scenario: You are in heaven. There is brilliance all around you, and you see and hear things far beyond anything depicted in any science-fiction film. There are four live aliens, and each time they ascribe praise and power to the One who sits on a dazzling throne, two-dozen leaders get off their seats of power and lay flat down at the foot of that throne. These rulers throw their crowns down. They worship profoundly.

How would you respond? Wouldn't it be hard to sit through all this unmoved?

Then you hear these leaders say something. Their majestic words swell through the courts of heaven, and what they say speaks to you. You hear them declare that the Just Judge is deserving of such extreme worship because the existence of all things is owed to Him. They are singing "The Creation Canticle."

SONG OF THE CREATED ONES

In the beginning when God created everything, His glory was manifested. The Creation is the ground of all of God's other acts of power. It is a manifestation of His wisdom and His love and forms the basis for our thanksgiving.

There was a time when these elders in Revelation did not exist, but by God's power they came to be out of nothing. So with gratitude they sing:

"You are worthy, our Lord and God, to receive glory and honor and power, for you created all things, and by your will they were created and have their being" (Rev. 4:11, NIV).

The "Creation Canticle" confirms the incomparable worthiness of their "Lord and God." It is interesting to note the historical background of the term "our Lord and God."[1] This was a popular term used in the Roman culture of the day to denote emperor worship. Emperor worship was required by some of the evil and self-centered Caesars, such as Nero, Caligula and Domitian. They wanted their divinity expressed while they were alive. People (especially Christians) who refused to attribute this term to Caesar were killed.

In the face of these emperors, John hears the leaders in heaven singing, "Our Lord and God," as if mocking all smaller earth potentates. The leaders of the courts of heaven use this Roman term in direct defiance of the worship of Caesar. It appears to be a clear rejection of the self-acclaimed deity of the Emperor Domitian.

The elders sing, "You are worthy to receive glory and honor and power."

"Glory" is the visible as well as the audible praise of His subjects.

"Honor" means "esteem" and "dignity."

"Power" is the supernatural, miracle-working power as attributed to the force of all things. He is worthy to receive power. He is merited with limitless power. We can confer no power to Him for we cannot add something to Him. However we can spend our power as we exalt His infinite power. I will praise him with *all* my strength.

CREATION THAT INSPIRES ADORATION

If we were totally honest, creation (and this includes human beings) knows that the Creator is deserving of absolute and total adoration in thought and action.

Creation was formed first in the mind of God before it ever existed. Then by His will, creation was fixed in place by His pleasure and came into being, and it continues by His maintenance. He is our Creator and that inspires to sing "The Creation Canticle."

It's interesting that the elders in Revelation declare, "You [God] created all things, and by Your *will* they exist and were created" (italics added). Man owes his existence to the will of God. Had God not willed us, we wouldn't be. Had God not desired us, we wouldn't be. We should be thankful. We should sing songs that give thanks to Him with a grateful heart. Lord, I give You thanks with a grateful heart, with an attitude of gratitude. Songwriter, write more songs of thankfulness and let us sing them to the Lord in the first person.

Therefore whatever we find in the universe whether wisdom, beauty, organic or mechanical, can be traced back to God and all the good is an expression of what was in Him in the beginning. All good and perfect gifts come from our Father above (see James 1:17). In fact, absolutely everything does.

WORRY'S ANSWER

This song speaks of God's infinitude. In eloquent simplicity, it states that prior to Creation nothing existed but God. Therefore all that is has its existence in God alone—everything in the heavens and earth, including the original form of Satan, fallen angels and spirits. He created it all. Nothing is out of control. There is One who sits on the throne and He rules and reigns. He is a great God. What He does, He does well.

Because of this we don't have to worry. Charles Simpson, prominent Bible teacher from Mobile, AL, once said, "Worry is a mild case of atheism!" We have a low view of God when we worry. Don't worry or be anxious for anything. God sits on the throne and He has all things in control. If we read the Scriptures on the greatness of God, it would defuse our anxiety.

> *"Worry is a mild case of atheism!"*

The purpose of Creation can be seen here in the short catechism. Man's chief end is to glorify God and enjoy Him forever. When this purpose is reversed and man's primary quest is to glorify himself and enjoy himself forever, we have problems. "God's will is perverted and sin comes into being," Jonathan Edwards says.[2] In this role the creation assumes the role of the Creator. This is seen in the worship of Caesars, artists and even worship leaders!

One of my friends for a short time was a worship leader at a church that prided themselves in their image and strived to excellence at the expense of integrity and character. One of the congregation's members introduced him to a friend as the "Elvis of our church." In his way he was honoring his worship leader but it exposed the paradigm of the church—how important image, notoriety and star status was.

MAKE GOD LARGE

The "Creation Canticle" is the conclusion of this great fifth chapter of Revelation—a transcendent and an introductory visit of John to heaven. The purpose of this song is to reveal the greatness and the grandeur of our God.

Worship leaders and pastors, part of your function is to reveal God as large as you can (though it won't be anywhere near what He really is!) You can't do it if you don't know the theology of God. You can't lead people to this level of worship if you are not a student of the Word or studying Christology.

If you do not yet understand God's attributes or nature, read books on the attributes of God. Read what the scholars and ancients wrote about who God is. Read the creeds and memorize them. Read the hymns and sing them. Write who God is. Sing songs that are anthems about the attributes of God. How can we sing anything but theology?

THRONES, GUITARS AND CROWNS

This portion of scripture reveals and foretells the beginning and the end of all creation. It leaves the visitor and the reader awestruck with reverence and deep worship. I get so inspired that my heart bursts in my chest every time I read this.

Heaven is open to John, and he saw the lightning play and the thunder dance. He saw the rainbow encircling the brilliant throne. He saw the visions of the great God Himself. In front of the seat of the Sovereign, the fires of the Holy Spirit forcibly flamed roaring with supernatural brilliance. Around the throne John saw the subordinate thrones on which sat the symbolic leaders of all the earth robed with white with crowns of victory on their heads, which they endlessly cast at the foot of the all-powerful Potentate.

Then spread out before the throne was a smooth expanse of a vast crystalline sea on which millions and millions of worshippers stood playing the "guitars of God." They sang to God a new song, original compositions that they had authored. Lift up your voice and

Heaven is open to John, and he saw the lightning play and the thunder dance. He saw the rainbow encircling the brilliant throne. He saw the visions of the great God Himself.

compose a new composition of the gratitude and the reverence and the thanksgiving of Him. This song arises to the Creator King.

Each time the four live aliens prescribe praise and power to the righteous Ruler, the two-dozen leaders get off their seats of power and lay down at the foot of the chair of the Just Judge. They declare He is deserving of such extreme worship, for we owe all existence to Him. He deserves all praise. He brought everything into existence out of nothing, and we are forever grateful. This they do continuously in heaven.

Likewise, we should worship 24/7, not just when we are at the church building. This we should do as part of the rhythm of our life in moanings and groanings, in sighs and cries.

OUR UTMOST FOR HIS HIGHEST

In songs and speech we give our acclamations, our proclamations, our declarations, our adorations and our venerations to Him. We give God our utmost for His highest. So whatever our profession, calling, talent and gifts may be, the Creator deserves all the adoration of all our hearts. He deserves all the power of our praise and all the worship of our lives, for we are His creation.

We should sing the "Creation Canticle" with those who have gone before and the aliens, the twenty-four leaders, all the angels, the seraphs, the cherubs, the overcomers and the great crowd of witnesses giving Him glory and honor. He is the great Creator, the sovereign Lord and we bless and praise Him.

We praise You, Father Creator. We thank You for creating us and making us dependent on You, though You have no need of us. We thank You for blessing all creatures with life. We magnify and extol You as the Creator who upholds all things by your unlimited power. We worship You because we are grateful to You for our life and existence.

---

[1] This term is translated "our Lord and God" in the NIV and is noted "our Lord and God" from the NU and M texts in the NKJV. (NKJV uses "O Lord" but in the notes states "Our Lord and God" is more accurate).

[2] Jonathan Edwards, *The Nature of True Virtue*, 261 (referenced in *Singing with Angels*, 43).

CHAPTER SIX

THE
LION LAMB

*And I saw in the right hand of Him who sat on the throne a scroll
written inside and on the back, sealed with seven seals.*

*Then I saw a strong angel proclaiming with a loud voice,
"Who is worthy to open the scroll and to loose its seals?"*

*And no one in heaven or on the earth or under the earth
was able to open the scroll, or to look at it.*

*So I wept much, because no one was found worthy
to open and read the scroll, or to look at it.*

*But one of the elders said to me, "Do not weep. Behold, the Lion of
the tribe of Judah, the Root of David, has prevailed to open
the scroll and to loose its seven seals."*

*And I looked, and behold, in the midst of the throne and
of the four living creatures, and in the midst of the elders, stood a
Lamb as though it had been slain. (Rev. 5:1-6a)*

Who is worthy? That burning question from heaven tore at
John's heart. In this chapter, you will take a look at the One who *is*
worthy and sing the song of the Redeemer.

THE KING AND THE SCROLL

*And I saw in the right hand of Him who sat on the throne a scroll
written inside and on the back, sealed with seven seals (Rev. 5:1).*

John said, "I saw." He had a vision and instantly observed
Yahweh sitting on His throne as King and Judge, ruling over all
things. God's right hand was open as if inviting someone to take its
contents, a message written on a closed scroll.

Some scholars theorize that this scroll might have been the
redemptive plan of all humanity—the plan of God, inaugurated in
Jesus Christ from before the beginning of time. It was written on
both sides, front and back, which was a very rare thing in this time of
history. Usually the back of the scroll was used for the address and
the addressee. Written on both sides indicates its message is full. It is
very possible this scroll is the Book of Life described in other verses
in Revelation and in Philippians 4:3.

The rolled up scroll was also sealed with seven seals. During
this time period, seals were made from hot wax. A person would drip

the hot wax on one side of the parchment, and the king would press his signet ring into the wax, leaving his signet impression on it. It was the mark of authenticity and authority. Then the same thing was done on the other side of the parchment, and they were tied together with a string. The strings could not be broken or loosened because the king had sealed them. Only the recipient could break the seals and open the scroll to read it. These seals were used on legal documents and were therefore "locked," as in Roman contracts or wills.

Note here that there was not one seal, but seven on this scroll. "Seven" is the number for completeness in the Bible. This scroll was completely closed and locked-up to ensure the security of its content.

SEALS AND TEARS

Then I saw a strong angel proclaiming with a loud voice, "Who is worthy to open the scroll and to loose its seals?" (Rev. 5:2)

This was not an average messenger from God, but a very large and powerful angel. Its strong and intense voice boomed as if using a giant megaphone: "*Who is worthy?*"

The word "worthy" here has the meaning of "weight." The angel is asking:

"Who has enough weight or substance to open this scroll?"

"Who has the value or worth to break the seals?"

"Who has the deservedness, substance or value?"

"Who is entitled or accomplished enough to take the scroll and unlock it?"

"Who among heaven and earth's creatures has enough merit to open this book?"

"Is there anyone who claims the right to open the book?"

In a great and mighty voice the messenger roared, "Who has the authority to come and to take the book out of the hand of King Yahweh and break the seven locks secured with the signet ring of God?"

There was no response to the angel's wrenching question. Everyone was silent in heaven.

> *"Who has the authority to come and to take the book out of the hand of King Yahweh and break the seven locks secured with the signet ring of God?"*

And no one in heaven or on the earth or under the earth was able to open the scroll, or to look at it (Rev. 5:3).

No one in heaven or on earth, in the terrestrial or the celestial, is qualified or able to execute God's redemptive plan that is contained in this scroll. No angel or cherub in heaven had the right even to look at the scroll, much less *open* it. On earth there was no person, creature or spirit who could read what was inside. Under the earth there was none among the dead deserving enough to receive the book and unlock its contents and read its message. None of these could even understand it or discern it.

John was so overwhelmed with this vision that he began to weep. His crying must have been gut wrenching.

So I wept much, because no one was found worthy to open and read the scroll, or to look at it (Rev. 5:4).

John didn't just use the word just "weep." He said, "I wept much." He wept and wept. The idea here is that this was loud wailing, as one would do at a funeral in the Middle East. John is inferring that he wept out loud with agonizing cries and screams when he saw no one deserving to unseal the secrets of God. So John was greatly grieved, and he began to cry and sob with bitter tears because the contents of the book will not be known. He thought the plan of God's redemption for all history was not going to be disclosed or His will executed.

THE LION KING

Then to John's surprise, one of the twenty-four elders in the heavenly court around God's throne spoke.

But one of the elders said to me, "Do not weep. Behold, the Lion of the tribe of Judah, the Root of David, has prevailed to open the scroll and to loose its seven seals" (Rev. 5:5).

Behold, look! The Lion of the tribe of Judah is able.

The lion is a symbol of dominion, authority and government. A lion is on Judah's banner. That is why He is called "the Lion of the tribe of Judah" because He has absolute dominion. All events are under His control. He is the King and Judge; He holds all authority and all rule. He is the supreme Commander of all things.

> "He *stripped* all the *spiritual tyrants* in the universe of their *sham authority* at the *Cross* and marched them *naked* through the *streets*."

Nowhere in the Bible before this point is Jesus referred to as a lion, the king of beasts. Jesus is the King of creation, the Monarch of the universe, the King of kings.

This is the lion that Jacob foresaw when he prophesied over his sons while blessing them. He called Judah a lion's whelp through which the scepter (a symbol of kingship) shall not depart until Shiloh comes. (See Gen. 49:9, 10.) This Lion King is of the tribe of Judah, indicating the genealogy of Jesus mentioned in Matthew, chapter one. When Jesus came, the lineage was changed from the tribe of Levi to that of Judah. (See Hebrews 7:11-14.) Verse fourteen of that passage says, "It is evident that our Lord arose from Judah."

Then there is the interesting phrase in Rev. 5:5 that Lion is the root of David. "Root" means the sprout, as a life-giving sprout would come out of a dead log lying in the middle of the forest. So

Jesus, who once was dead in the middle of humanity's forest, sprouted to life.

This Lion King is of the family tree of David. David died as all men do. Today, you can visit a tomb on Mt. Zion that may very well be David's tomb. Out of that throne, out of that deadness, comes a new life. Luke 1:31-32 says, "...Call His name JESUS. He will be great, and will be called the Son of the Highest; and the Lord God will give Him the throne of His father David." This Lion King "has the key of David, He who opens and no one shuts, and shuts and no one opens" (Rev. 3:7).

The "Lion...has prevailed." This is a powerful statement because it references what Jesus did from the Crucifixion to the Resurrection. The NIV translates this phrase, the "Lion...has triumphed." The Lion spoiled principalities and powers and robbed them of their prey. Then He made an example of them by putting them to open shame. In full display, He shattered their power, emptying and totally defeating them. He celebrated at their expense His triumphal act at the Cross. The Message says it this way: "He stripped all the spiritual tyrants in the universe of their sham authority at the Cross and marched them naked through the streets" (Col. 2:15).

When Christ died He descended into the lower parts of hell. The Bible says, "Having disarmed the powers and authorities, he made a public spectacle of them, triumphing over them by the cross"

(Col. 2:15, NIV). Jesus triumphed over the dark powers by loosing the prisoners in hell, taking them captive, and gloriously leading them to heaven. It was like He said, "Come on boys, we are going on a march for Jesus!" And then He proceeded out of hell and up to terra firma where they displayed their victory. Hundreds were seen who had come back to life.

After Jesus rose from the grave, He said that He was going to ascend to His Father. True to His word, He did just that. His followers watched Him rise high into the heavens until He disappeared. He sat down at the right hand of His Majesty on high. His redemptive work was finished. (See John 20:17; Acts 1:9-11; Ephesians 1:20; John 19:30.)

Jesus' followers were told He would come again. Like them, we wait with expectation. This is the centerpiece of our worship. Jesus is Judah's lion, the King of the spirit world, the Lion of the lords.

THE LAMB KING

And I looked, and behold, in the midst of the throne and of the four living creatures, and in the midst of the elders, stood a Lamb as though it had been slain (Rev. 5:6a).

A lion is the ultimate symbol of power. A lamb is a symbol of powerlessness. Jesus was a Lion-Lamb. A lion and a lamb stand in stark contrast to the other. They are opposites. What a mystery! The lamb signifies gentleness and sacrifice. Many scholars say this speaks of the Passover lamb.

It is interesting to note that while other parts of the New Testament do reference Jesus as a lamb, the term doesn't occur frequently there. (See John 1:29, 36; Acts 8:32-35; 1 Peter 1:19.) However, in the Apocalypse, Jesus as the Lamb is used frequently. The Lamb is the centerpiece of worship in heaven. If He is the center of worship, then it is important to contemplate the passion of the Christ:

He bears the wounds of the violent slaughter.

"He grew up before him like a tender shoot, and like a root out of dry ground, He had no beauty or majesty to attract us to him, nothing in his appearance that we should desire him. He was despised and rejected by men, a man of sorrows, and familiar with suffering. Like one from whom men hide their faces he was despised, and we esteemed him not. Surely he took up our infirmities and carried our sorrows, yet we considered him stricken by God, smitten by him, and afflicted. But he was pierced for our transgressions, he was crushed for our iniquities; the punishment that brought us peace was upon him, and by his wounds we are healed. We all, like sheep, have gone astray, each of us has turned to his own way; and the LORD has laid on him the iniquity of us all. He was oppressed and afflicted, yet he did not open his mouth; he was led like a lamb to the slaughter, and as a sheep before her shearers is silent, so he did not open his mouth. By oppression and judgment he was taken away. And who can speak of his descendants? For he was cut off from the land of the living; for the transgression of my people he was stricken. He was assigned a grave with the wicked and with the rich in his death, though he had done no violence, nor was any deceit in his mouth" (Is. 53:2-9, NIV).

It was John the Baptist who boldly said, "Behold the Lamb of God!" (John 1:36). The wondrous work of the great Redeemer is finished. He has made atonement for the sin of all humankind.

Most of the time, a lamb is portrayed in Christian art as a cute, white, stuffed beanie-baby toy. However this Lamb was red with blood. He appeared with the crimson stream of His slaughter and the cuts of His murder. This Lamb who was maliciously murdered is very much alive, but He bears the wounds of the violent slaughter. Perhaps the Lamb has these marks in heaven to give us evidence that this is the "Lamb slain from the foundation of the world" (Rev. 13:8).

Remember what Thomas said about Jesus after His resurrection? "Unless I see in His hands the print of the nails, and put my finger into the print of the nails, and put my hand into His side, I will not believe" (John 20:25). Then, after seeing and feeling the marks of His slaughter, he cried, "My Lord and my God!" (v. 28).

And so this Lamb Lion in heaven is marked with the evidence of His sacrificial slaughter so all may see and be reminded of His sacrifice.

Good news! The slain Lamb was not *lying* on the ground as a lifeless lump. He was *standing!* This word "stood" in this verse indicates that He has triumphed as victor over the death's dark dominion. He has subdued hell, and He rose from the grave. He is raised to stand upright, and this is the evidence that He conquered and triumphed. What a beautiful picture. He was killed, yes, but now alive and standing tall. His upright posture is saying, "I was cut down but they could not finally kill me."

> *"Look! I see the heavens opened and the Son of Man standing at the right hand of God!"*

When Stephen was being stoned for his faith, and his spirit began to cross over to the other side, he saw the Lord standing. He cried, "Look! I see the heavens opened and the Son of Man standing at the right hand of God!" (Acts 7:56). Jesus was not lying down, but standing in victory!

Doesn't this make you want to worship? Then do so. Give the Lion Lamb the glory and praise He deserves. It is Christ crucified and risen that we worship.

Holy abandon, passionate grace

Flowing along with the blood from your face

Seen from a distance, looked on with fear

Ultimate sacrifice to draw us near

At the cross lies the hope of the world

At the cross where dreams lay unfurled

At the cross is the victory won

Life does not end, it's begun at the cross

Seemed like a failure, all hope was lost

Death cried triumphantly, "Where is your God?"

The whole earth was shaken with no one to save

When out of the darkness you conquered the grave

At the cross lies the hope of the world

At the cross where dreams lay unfurled

At the cross is the victory won

Life does not end, it's begun at the cross[1]

---

[1] Bethany Baroni, "At the Cross" © *2003 Glory Alleluia Music.*

CHAPTER SEVEN

THE
SONG OF
REDEMPTION

*Stood a Lamb as though it had been slain, having seven horns
and seven eyes, which are the seven Spirits of God sent out into
all the earth. Then He came and took the scroll out of the
right hand of Him who sat on the throne.*

*Now when He had taken the scroll, the four living creatures and the
twenty-four elders fell down before the Lamb, each having a harp, and
golden bowls full of incense, which are the prayers of the saints.*

*And they sang a new song, saying:
"You are worthy to take the scroll,
And to open its seals;
For You were slain,
And have redeemed us to God by Your blood
Out of every tribe and tongue and people and nation,*

And have made us kings and priests to our God;
And we shall reign on the earth."
(Revelation 5:6b-10)

We have come to a breathtaking moment in heaven. God is on His brilliant throne, a sealed scroll in His right hand representing His will of redemption for humankind. Awe-inspiring celestial beings surround the throne and worship the One who lives forever and ever. An angel in a thunderous voice asks who is worthy to open and read the scroll. Silence. No one in heaven has the authority to open the scroll or even to look at it. John weeps. He must have thought, *Oh no, nobody is worthy. The book will be sealed forever. We are doomed!*

Then hope is born. The slain Lamb of God, the Lord Jesus Christ, has prevailed and will open the scroll. The Lamb stands in their midst and takes the scroll. Jesus Christ is not laying down a murdered mess, but He stands, triumphant over death, hell and the grave. He stands triumphant over every power. Every full, complete work is His victory. He stands at the center. When John said, "Behold the Lamb," he was saying, "Behold the Cross! Behold the Passover Lamb. Behold the forgiveness of sins."

The "Song of Redemption" and the other songs in the Apocalypse reveal what worship is really like in the eternal realm. Worship is truer and more real there than what our worship is on this side. As we hear redemption's song, we are inspired to make our worship pure as we praise the One who died for us.

THE LAMB'S POWER AND PERCEPTION

The slain Lamb bore the slaughter marks of His sacrifice. He was bloodied, yet not beaten, and He was standing to proclaim victory to those He has redeemed and to the hosts in heaven. The Lamb had seven horns and seven eyes. The picture seems odd to us, but its symbolism has poignant and powerful meaning:

> *Stood a Lamb as though it had been slain, having*
> *seven horns and seven eyes, which are the seven*
> *Spirits of God sent out into all the earth (Rev. 6b).*

"Seven" signifies completeness and "horn" the power and the authority of God. It could be said that the seven horns symbolize perfect power or the omnipotence of the Lamb. The Lamb King has complete strength, dominion and fullness of power.

"Seven eyes" speak of the complete discerning Spirit of God and symbolize the perfect wisdom or the omniscience of the Lamb. He is the all-knowing, all-perceiving and all-seeing Holy Spirit. Complete in His perfect understanding and insight, He is able to survey all things simultaneously.

These seven Spirits of God were sent out into all the earth. They symbolize the perfect omnipresence of the Lamb. The sevenfold, complete fullness of the Holy Spirit is perfect in His worldwide endeavors. The Holy Spirit is working absolutely everywhere!

Some think God is not working in primitive cultures until the first missionaries arrive. That simply is not true. The Holy Spirit has gone out into all the earth drawing people to God. He does not fundamentally need man to evangelize but does commission and use man to do so. The operation of the Holy Spirit is complete, moving in all people groups.

> *Then He came and took the scroll out of the right hand*
> *of Him who sat on the throne (Rev. 5:7).*

The Lamb comes and takes the scroll out of the open hand of Yahweh sitting on the throne because He is worthy to read it. The earthly counterpart to this heavenly scroll is a last will and testament. In the Roman culture, a will could not be opened until the death of the person. Also, under Roman law a document was valid only when the addressee had received it. This official will was written by Yahweh and possibly addressed to Jesus. It could not be opened until Jesus died. Since the Lamb died but now lives, He can open His own will for humankind and read it.

THE ALIENS, THE ELDERS AND THEIR GUITARS

> *Now when He had taken the scroll, the four living creatures*
> *and the twenty-four elders fell down before the Lamb, each*
> *having a harp, and golden bowls full of incense, which are*
> *the prayers of the saints (Rev. 5:8).*

Who are these four living creatures and twenty-four elders? The four aliens were possibly lower than man but higher than animals, so they were some kind of extra-celestial creatures. "Four" typifies a universal number; in earth there are the four winds, four seasons, four corners of the earth. The universality of these four living creatures speaks of all creation or all kingdoms, animal, vegetable, mineral, etc.

The twenty-four elders were the ruling judges or counselors. Elders were wise men as in the Jewish community who were called upon to make wise decisions. They had a governmental and priestly function here in heaven as well. The number "twenty-four" symbolizes the twenty-four orders of priests. These elders had gathered all around the action like elders would be at the Eucharist in Holy Communion.

They got low down, ***flat down,*** *and lay down before the* ***Holy One*** *on the throne.*

When the Lamb took the scroll, the aliens and the elders fell down before Him. There is a cause-and-effect here. When the Bible says they "fell down" it implies that they took a posture of profound worship. They got low down, flat down, and lay down before the Holy One on the throne. These leaders (very possibly they are sitting on thrones at this moment) got up and fell down in extreme obeisance. The picture here is that all creatures from all corners of the earth and all leaders and rulers are to prostrate themselves in worship before the Lamb who is the King.

Each one of these twenty-four had a harp. The literal word in Greek is *kithara*, "a lute or guitar." It didn't look like a harp like we think of it today. Historically it was triangular in shape, with seven strings (later increased to eleven). Josephus says it had ten, and was played with a "plectrum" or a pick made of ivory.[1] These harps represent the worship music of the Levitical temple choir that speaks of prophetic worship.

———•·•———

*Paying in blood you **bought men**.*

———•·•———

The aliens and the elders were holding bowls (vials). The bowls could be described as low-cut vases, flat vessels, used for boiling liquids or for drinking. These "golden incense-cups" were used to receive frankincense, which was lighted with coals from the brazen altar and offered on the golden altar before the veil. An image here is from the temple and tabernacle service and refers to the altar of incense, praise and prayer.[2]

These bowls were "full of incense, which are the prayers of the saints." Fragrant powder, possibly contrited stone, was burned in worship. Some of us were rocks honed out of the quarry of humanity—arrogant and haughty. Then we met the Solid Rock, and He broke us up and made us as talcum powder. We shouldn't forget the process of contrited stone; it is the essence and purity of true worship.

THE CONTINUING CELESTIAL CANTICLE

John, the liturgist, says, "And they sang a new song." This is a picture of heaven's perpetual worship. The new song is in the present tense giving the meaning of continuous, unceasing music. It was of a new kind, fresh, instantaneous, recently made, unused, unworn, unprecedented, uncommon and never heard before song. Songs like these were sung in the temple when worship leaders composed spontaneously inspired psalms called "spiritual songs."

The theme of this new song is redemption. This song of redemption is different from other songs. One would never have needed to sing this song if man had not fallen and the Redeemer had not redeemed him.

And they sang a new song, saying:

> *"You are worthy to take the scroll,*
> *And to open its seals;*
> *For You were slain,*
> *And have redeemed us to God by Your blood*
> *Out of every tribe and tongue and people and nation" (Rev. 5:9).*

PURCHASED TO WORSHIP

Note that the song says, "You...have redeemed us to God by Your blood." Another version says, "With your blood you purchased men for God" (NIV). The language is of atonement. The lyric could read, "Paying in blood you bought men." Jesus wasn't just a martyr, a good teacher who died. He was God-in-flesh man who lay down His life as a victim for all humankind to satisfy the requirements of the law. God gratuitously through His grace made us in right standing with Him by buying us with the currency of the blood of His son Jesus. This satisfied the requirements of the law and now God accepts as righteous those who have faith in Jesus (Rom. 3:24-26).

Jesus redeemed men and women from everywhere. He has no favorites. He bought people from every *tribe, tongue, people and nation.*

"Tribe" here is a small company of people associated with an ancestor. It is a group of people like a family or a race having a common ancestor such as a tribe of Israel or a tribe of Indians.

He also redeemed us "out of every…tongue." This is a division of humanity's family that is larger than a tribe but all speak the same language. "Every tongue" is a picture of all those who speak all languages on the face of the earth.

It doesn't stop there. He redeemed us "out of every…people." This is a larger group than a tribe or language. It's a mass of people made up of smaller divisions—a multitude of bodies united together such as an army and made up of regiments or battalions. It could be a mass of people made up of societies and guilds, various trades or professions. This is a picture of "every people," no matter what people-group. No one will be excluded from the blessings of redemption.

The list concludes with "out of every…nation." A nation is a larger and wider group. It means a nation under one sovereign rule such as the British nation with Anglo-Saxon, Scottish, Irish, Welsh, etc. The sense is that the blessings of redemption will be extended to all parts of the earth. God's family transcends all cultures, all linguistic, racial and national boundaries and borders. The gospel has reached to all strata of society, even to the outermost parts of the earth. God has purchased the souls of persons from every part of all divisions of humanity that they might worship Him.

> *God has purchased the souls of persons from every part of all divisions of humanity that they might worship Him.*

A WAR PARTY WORSHIPS

A story is told of Reverend I. P. Scott, a pioneer missionary to India. In one of his journeys to an unreached area, he came upon a war party. They seized him and pointed their spears to his heart. Feeling utterly helpless and not knowing what else to do, he took out his violin and began to play. He sang in their native language, "All hail the power of Jesus name." As the music and lyrics rang out, he closed his eyes fearing death would come at any moment. But when nothing happened even after the third verse, he opened his eyes and was amazed to see that they had dropped their spears and their eyes were filled with tears. They invited him to their homes and for several years he worked among them leading many to Christ.[3]

VERTICAL CALL

And [You] have made us kings and priests to our God;
and we shall reign on the earth (Rev. 5:10).

We are bought by His blood to be royal priests. The NIV translates this verse "You have made them to be a kingdom and priests to serve our God." We are not to serve our needs or other people; what we do is in service to God. As you lead worship, grasp the fact that you are not a priest to people. The highest ministry isn't to minister to people, whether in sermon or song, but to the Lord. When it's time to worship, we sing songs to Him because we are priests to God: "To Him who loved us and washed us from our sins in His own blood, and has made us kings and priests to His God and Father, to Him be glory and dominion forever and ever. Amen" (Rev. 1:5b-6).

The "Song of Redemption" concludes with the line, "And we shall reign on the earth." The dominion on the earth will be given to saints. "They will prevail in the rule of God, and the redeemed will govern the affairs of the nations" is what this little phrase means. The followers of Christ will be everywhere reigning with the authority of Christ. I don't have a timeline chart for this. I don't really know when these things will be and exactly what will happen, but as long as I follow Jesus, it will work out.

HEAVEN'S PRAISE GATHERING

The Dead Sea Scrolls indicate that earthly worshipers of the first century envisioned themselves participating with the angels in heavenly worship when they read this song. They went vertical. They joined the crowd of witnesses, the four living aliens, the twenty-four elders, the one hundred and forty-four thousand and all the overcomers standing on the crystal sea with the harps of God.

All races, peoples, nations, generations and denominations will stand before Him and sing new compositions.

You see, worship is all about Him, His space and little about us. He is the initiator, the giver of redemption and we are the recipients. Therefore every tongue, tribe, people and nation will stand before Him and sing in worship to Him. All races, peoples, nations, generations and denominations will stand before Him and sing new compositions.

The Apocalypse—the revelation of Jesus Christ—is transcendent and revealing. In it you sense the spirit of the music from the other side. One almost hears the elders playing guitars with the innumerable company of guitar players on the crystal sea. This is the perpetual praise of heaven:

> *And they sang a new song, saying:*
> *"You are worthy to take the scroll, and to open its seals;*
> *for You were slain, and have redeemed us to God by*
> *Your blood out of every tribe and tongue and people and nation,*
> *and have made us kings and priests to our God; and*
> *we shall reign on the earth."*

WHAT TO DO ABOUT IT

Perhaps you have come through tempest and trouble. It's been a hard year and lots of chains are jiggling behind you reminding you of your limitations. However, you want to go on this journey, but you are too encumbered and heavy in your spirit. Before you can go higher where the air is cleaner and the view is clearer, you have to lay the rest aside. Find a posture that is appropriate in these next few moments. Join the realm of angels and elders. Go vertical and say *"Father, I lay it all down at the feet of the bloodied Lamb. Jesus is the Lamb that was slain for my sins that I may be able to sing the song of the redeemed."*

[1] *Vincent's Word Studies in the New Testament*, Electronic Database, Copyright © 1997 by Biblesoft. (*Kithara*, NT:2788).

[2] *Vincent's Word Studies in the New Testament*, Electronic Database, Copyright © 1997 by Biblesoft.

[3] Louis Albert Banks, *Immortal Hymns and Their Stories* (Cleveland, OH, Burrows Brother, 1898), 312-313.

CHAPTER EIGHT

ANGELS

*Then I looked and heard the voice of many angels, numbering
thousands upon thousands, and ten thousand times ten thousand.
(Rev. 5:11)*

Have you ever wondered what angels sing about?

That is an important question to ask, for we can learn
something from the songs of these creatures on the other side. Billy
Graham once said, "I believe that angels have the capacity to employ
heavenly celestial music. In heaven we will be taught the language
and music of the celestial world."[1] The Apocalypse gives us clues to
how angels worship and what they sing.

WHAT ARE ANGELS LIKE?

Angels are a mystery. They intrigue us. Go into any secular
bookstore, and you will see numerous books on angels and
supernatural beings. Never before have I seen such a hunger for the

supernatural! And yet, despite the proliferation of information about angels, the world is misinformed about what the Bible says about them.

Angels are a special order of supernatural or heavenly beings created by God. They do not look like humans with wings as depicted in so much Christian art. They are celestial spirits, immortal, and embodied creatures. In other words, they are spirits that have a body or form.

Angels are like the wind and flaming lightening. They have power to move things and transport quickly.

Angels can and do manifest in a form like humans, although usually they are invisible to the human eye. There are times, however, that angels are seen in clothing that is so white and brilliant that they terrify humans. Abraham saw angels as did Hagar, Lot, Jacob, Moses, Balaam, Joshua, Gideon, Manoah, David, Elijah, Elisha, Daniel, Zechariah, Mary, Joseph, Zechariah, shepherds, Peter, John, Philip, Cornelius, Paul and John. Even a donkey and a lion in the Bible saw an angel! (See Gen. 18:2; Gen. 19:1; Ps. 103:20; Luke 24:4.)

Holy angels never lost their created glory through sin like we did. Therefore, they do not need redemption. They can't sing the song of the redeemed, but they do have particular interest in the salvation of people in the world. They watch with excited anticipation the divine expression of God's love extended to earthlings. They rejoice when humans believe in Jesus Christ. (See Luke 15:10; 1 Peter 1:12.)

WHAT DO ANGELS DO?

Angels are messengers or agents of God to fulfill divine will. (See Acts 10:3-7, 22; Job 33:23.) Angels were connected with Jesus' life on earth. The Gospels are full of accounts of angels as they announced His birth (Luke 1:26; Matt. 1:20), directed His flight to Egypt (Matt. 2:13, 22), and ministered to Him in the desert (Matt. 4:11). Angels strengthened Him while in prayer in Gethsemane (Luke 22:43) and rolled away the stone of His grave (Matt. 28:2). They told the good news of His Resurrection and assured the disciples of His Ascension. Angels were present as Jesus entered heaven, and angels will accompany Him on His glorious return. (See Acts 1:10; Matt. 16:27; 2 Thess. 1:7.)

Angels are ministering spirits sent to help those who are believers. Although the idea of each person having a "guardian angel" is not really found in Scripture, angels assist God in answering a believer's prayers. Angels position themselves near and around those that fear the Lord and they protect them. (See Hebrews 1:14; Ps. 91:11, 12; Acts 5:19.)

Angels are like the wind and flaming lightening. They have power to move things and transport quickly. They are meek, wise and some are extremely powerful. They are not, however, all-powerful and all-knowing, like God. (See Ps. 104:4; Ps. 103:20; 2 Thess. 1:7.)

The Bible also says the Lord is among the angels. God is called the Lord of hosts (Jehovah Sabaoth), which means the Commander of all the armies (hosts) of heaven. Angels exercise influence in the physical realm when commanded by God. There was an occasion that God told David in battle, "When you hear a sound of marching in the tops of the mulberry trees, then you shall go out to battle, for God has gone out before you" (1 Chron. 14:15; see also 2 Sam. 5:24). Scholars say that the sound of marching here is not sound of wind, but the sound of an army advancing. David's instructions were to wait with his earthly army until God's celestial army began to move. It is interesting that angels are also called the "chariots of God" because of their strength and their ability to move quickly as mighty war vehicles. (See Ps. 68:17.)

Angels stand on the right and left sides of God's throne. Angels play musical instruments and worship endlessly.

Angels proclaim and execute God's judgments. An angel pronounced judgment on King Herod and struck him with worms because he wouldn't give glory to God. Angels destroyed wicked Sodom. An angel destroyed Israel with a pestilence; 70,000 people died of sickness. An angel destroyed the Assyrian army by killing 185,000 men. The Bible says that angels will separate the wicked from the good and cast them in the furnace of fire. (See Acts 12:23; Gen. 19:13; 2 Sam. 24:15; Matt. 13:41, 42.)

Angels stand on the right and left sides of God's throne. Angels play musical instruments and worship endlessly, which is their primary function. It is not surprising then that the Revelation of Jesus Christ is full of angels. *Perhaps this book's disclosure of the praises to God sung by these heavenly hosts will motivate us to worship Him!* (See 1 Kings 22:19; Ps. 148:1, 2; Rev. 8:2.)

WORSHIP MACHINES

With all their importance, angels are careful to point out they are created beings and forbid worship of themselves (Rev. 22:8, 9). Whenever they appear, they point our gaze up to God.

There is a place for horizontal ministry and even performance when ministering to people. This, in a narrow sense, is not worship. But don't make the mistake of calling your performance of practiced pieces worship. Worship is for our Lord, not for people. It is meant to be vertical. The example of angels not allowing themselves to be worshiped is a warning to us. Worship leaders should not allow the congregation to be "star-struck." They should tell people as the angels do, "Look up, don't focus on me, worship Jesus!"

SUPERNATURAL SOLDIERS

Probably the most familiar display of angels on earth took place at Jesus' birth: "An angel of the Lord stood before them [the shepherds], and the glory of the Lord shone around them, and they were greatly afraid…And suddenly there was with the angel a multitude of the heavenly host praising God and saying: 'Glory to God in the highest, and on earth peace, good will toward men!'" (Luke 2:9, 13, 14).

Luke says the angel of the Lord caused shepherds to be extremely afraid. When people truly see angels, they shouldn't be nonchalant about it. Sometimes people say, "I saw this angel yesterday," as if it were no big deal. My response to that is, "And you lived to tell about it?" I wonder if what they really saw was an angel. Many times in the Bible when people met an angel, the first thing the angel said was "Don't be afraid!" Could the reason be because the people were so terrified at the awesome presence of these powerful creatures?

Luke also says this visitation happened unexpectedly. The angels didn't come down the road like the headlights of a Chevy approaching in the distance while the shepherds said, "Forsooth brethren, here comes the angel of the Lord." Then they could have prepared themselves for a visitation. Remember there was no electricity then. The night was very dark, and the flicker of the campfire was what the shepherds used for light. Scripture says the angels appeared "suddenly," not "by and by." God is very dramatic. When God-encounters occur, the experience is dramatic and sometimes traumatic.

There was a celestial army of luminaries marching from the sky that were lauding and boasting of God in a prepared piece of music.

Not only was the appearance of angels totally unexpected and awe-inspiring, there were huge numbers of them ("a multitude of the heavenly host"). This means there was a celestial army of luminaries marching from the sky that were lauding and boasting of God in a prepared piece of music. Troops and troops of supernatural soldiers, celestial luminaries, suddenly lit up the sky!

The angels were "praising God," extolling or singing the praise and honor of God. These angels revealed themselves to earthlings and were totally focused on the eternal realm of Adonai (their Lord and Master). They did not come to sing to men, though the men heard their song—they were praising God.

Angels don't sing for our "listening pleasure" with a musical piece that they have prepared. Rather, the angels are captivated by what happens around the throne. Why aren't we? The angels sing glory to God; their worship is vertical. Even though these angels came "down," their worship went "up."

"Glory to God in the highest!" shout the angels. Their praises ascend to the Most High in the highest regions. I just want to explode in praise and worship when I read that text. Let's praise Him now with this angel anthem.

ANGEL SIGHTINGS

Dwayne and Sue Kershner were hosting a meeting in the state of Oaxaca, Mexico. There was an unusual lethargy in the gathering probably due to the weather and the condition of the building. It was very hot, about 106° outside and very dusty. The church building had a dirt floor and a roof made of banana leaves. The ceiling was so close to our heads that when you raised your hands you would prick your fingers! As we worshipped we sensed the spirit of joy in the place, but not everyone seemed to be joyful.

Suddenly a small young man in a simple white and hemless garment jumped up and danced an unusual dance. His movements and spirit captivated us. Immediately, everyone felt free and began to rejoice before the Lord. The women came forward and danced in circles, and the men jumped until their shirts were drenched with perspiration.

So many people were dancing that it produced a cloud of dust that shut down my amplifier. It was so dusty I could write my name on my guitar. It was very painful to breathe but it was a wonderful time!

When we looked for the dancing "worship leader," no one could find him. He had disappeared! We asked the pastors at the meeting if they knew who this young man was and where he came from, but no one knew him. This was unusual, for we were in a place where everybody knew everyone. We had chills when we were told this—chills similar to what we felt when he had danced. I don't know if it was an angel, but it was the closest I have been to a heavenly visitation of one. What I *do* know is that this young man in simple clothing pointed the direction of our worship heavenward. Such as it is in heaven!

Monks for centuries would sing continual praises to God and have visions of angels

MONK SONGS

Keep in mind that heaven is the place of perpetual praise. We see this clearly as we stand back and study the whole scene of worship in the Apocalypse. In our last chapter, we looked at the song that was sung by the four living creatures and the twenty-four elders praising the Lamb of God (Rev. 5:9, 10). Then, as soon as the song ended, the angels picked up the songs of praise in verse eleven: John said, "Then I looked, and I heard the voice of many angels around the throne."

Some medieval monasteries had customs that remind us that praise and worship is not to cease. When I was in Belfast, Ireland, I heard there was a beautiful cathedral that sits in a gorgeous valley called the "Valley of Angels." It is reported the valley is so named because monks for centuries would sing continual praises to God and have visions of angels as a result.

There is also a story told of a monastery that was overrun by a band of Norse raiders. They marched into this monastery and slaughtered the monks without mercy, even the ones who were singing praises to God. It had been the monks' practice to keep the vocal worship of God going continually. During the raid one of the monks was able to escape and hide in an inaccessible spot where the attackers were not likely to find him. But when this monk-in-hiding heard the sound of praises cease as the other monks were killed, instinctively he took up the song. When he did, he knew he would be betraying his hiding place. He was found and killed, but he would not keep silent.

Oh, that we would have a continuum of consistent worship and praise to Jesus Christ. May the song in our homes and our hearts never cease. Whether we are walking in the academic halls, riding or driving in our cars on the way to work or school, we should constantly worship. Why would we do this? Because we don't *go to* church, we *are* the church.

Paul instructed, "Do you not know that your body is the temple of the Holy Spirit?" (1 Corinthians 6:19). Worship goes on inside of temples. We don't go to a temple to worship. We *are* temples! So let's worship! People need to know this truth so that when we come together all a worship leader has to say is, "You ready to worship?" "Yeah," we say and instantly worship arises to God because that is what we live to do. We shouldn't need worship "prompters." We just need to maintain a life of worship!

THE CONTINUING CANTATA

The example is clear. Angels and all extra-celestials in heaven exist to worship God continually. As we see in Revelation, when the song of the elders and the living creatures concludes, praise is picked up by another source—the angels: Then I [John] looked, and I heard the voice of many angels around the throne (Rev. 5:11).

This continuum of song proceeds forever on the other side.

It is an example to us today. The psalmist says:

*"The Lord has established His throne in heaven, and His kingdom
rules over all. Bless the Lord, you His angels, who excel in strength,
who do His word, heeding the voice of His word. Bless the Lord,
all you His hosts [armies], you ministers of His, who do His pleasure.
Bless the Lord, all His works, in all places of His dominion.
Bless the Lord, O my soul!" (Ps. 103:19-22)*

---

[1] Dr. David Jeremiah, *What the Bible Says About Angels* (Multnomah, Sisters, OR, 1996), 105.

CHAPTER NINE

THE ANGEL ANTHEM

They encircled the throne and the living creatures
and the elders. In a loud voice they sang:
"Worthy is the Lamb, who was slain,
to receive power and wealth and wisdom and strength
and honor and glory and praise!"
(Rev. 5:11, 12, NIV)

Worship by angels transcends time and space. It does not involve giddy or sentimental feelings of nostalgia and metaphoric vagaries. Their song, recorded for us in the Apocalypse, expresses their deepest desire to see the Lord in all His glory. This "Angel Anthem" is mysterious, powerful, awesome and majestic as all of heaven joins in.

THE ANGELIC CHOIR

Then I looked and heard the voice of many angels, numbering thousands upon thousands, and ten thousand times ten thousand. They encircled the throne and the living creatures and the elders (Rev. 5:11, NIV).

John said simply that he "looked"; he discerned and discovered something majestic in its scope. As he looked, he also heard the roar of many voices resounding loudly in his ears. It was the sound of a large army of angels. These celestial creatures were worship beings, and out of their mouths loud praise flowed.

John said the angel choir numbered thousands upon thousands and ten thousand times ten thousand. When I was younger I thought this was a mathematical equation. So I would multiply ten thousand times ten thousand and then add a thousand thousands. However this is not a literal number of 101 million.

This is a term that suggests an innumerable multitude or an unlimited number. Ten thousand was the single largest number used in the Greek numerical system. Ten thousand times ten thousand meant it was an incalculable number. In other words, John was saying the number of these angels was beyond his ability to count!

This scene is similar to what Daniel described of a vast host in heaven ministering to God. "As I looked, thrones were set in place, and the Ancient of Days [God] took his seat... *Thousands upon thousands attended him; ten thousand times ten thousand* stood before him. The court was seated, and the books were opened" (Dan. 7:9, 10, NIV, italics added). The panoramic sight of innumerable hosts of worshippers must have inspired great wonder—both for Daniel and John!

Here in Revelation, myriads of angels sound as one single voice indicating a harmony of emotion and feelings as they lifted up their song in antiphonal praise. Then the Bible says, "They encircled the throne and the living creatures and the elders." John saw the angels on all sides of the center of activity. The throne and the Lamb were central, but around them were the aliens and the elders forming an inner circle. Around that was an outer circle of angels—an incalculable number of angels in this huge mass choir.

What instrument should we use to praise Yahweh that is equivalent to His most excellent greatness?

In a loud voice they sang: Worthy is the Lamb (Rev. 5:12a, NIV).

The innumerable company of angels lifted up their voice as a megaphone and sang very loudly, "Worthy is the Lamb." Their proximity and perception of the greatness of God required the appropriate praise. *Great is the Lord!* Guess how you are to praise Him. Greatly! He is not your "average" God (where you've seen one, you've seen them all!). He's the "God among the gods" and the "King among the kings." His praise should be louder than the praise of any other god.

The Bible says in Psalm 150:2 that we are to "Praise Him according to His excellent greatness." Now how are we going to do that? What instrument should we use to praise Yahweh that is equivalent to His most excellent greatness? Would we tinkle on a small triangle? Would we play a violin or a guitar? Floor toms and bass drums would not portray God equal to His greatness. Perhaps cannons or fireworks would work. No! None of these come close to being equivalent to His greatness. Yet I will spend my life trying to worship Him with all my strength and power!

WHAT ANGELS SING

Notice the majestic lyrics of the angels' song: "Worthy is the Lamb." They do not sing about the fire from the "Fire Conference" or the river from the "River CD." They do not sing abstract concepts or metaphors. They don't sing coy and cute songs to God. Angels don't sing about earthlings and our problems as we do. They sing about the attributes and character of God.

The reason why so many people in the pop culture cannot find stability in their lives is because our songs do not present Jesus on the Cross or on the throne. We settle for the man-centered songs of the "lowlands" which keeps our perspective horizontal. When we have a low view of God, we have a low worship. And today much of our worship is for our benefit—it's for our pleasure. We go home after worship and say, "I didn't get anything out of that." Our worship is not supposed to be a "feel-good" for us. Worship is for His eyes only—our utmost for the highest.

The worship and music of the other side is all about the Mysterious and the Majestic. When we contemplate and meditate on the greatness of God, *then* we can sing in worship how great He really is. Let the regal words of this classic worship song resonate in your heart—"How great Thou Art":

> *"Oh Lord my God, when I in awesome wonder,*
> *Consider all the worlds Thy hands have made.*
> *I see the stars, I hear the rolling thunder,*
> *Thy power throughout the universe displayed!*
> *Then sings my soul, my Savior God, to Thee;*
> *How great Thou art, How great Thou Art!"*[1]

Our souls sing when we "see" Him large and captivated by this awesome mystery and unspeakable majesty—not when the worship leader commands us to sing. These angels in Revelation are so captivated and caught-up with the Lamb of God that they sang all about Him. They sang with power and force. They sang with great effort, affection and emotion.

THE PASSION OF THE CHRIST

The angels do not address the Lamb directly. They do not sing to the Lamb, but sing of the Lamb, declaring in song a sevenfold tribute to the Lamb who was slain:

"Worthy is the Lamb, who was slain, to receive power and wealth and wisdom and strength and honor and glory and praise!"
(Rev. 5:11, 12, NIV)

"Worthy" is first word they sing. We sing this word so often and don't stop to think what it means. "Worthy" means having weight or substance. We could sing, "Deserving is the Lamb."

The word "Lamb" suggests a tender, young little lamb. But this Lamb was slain. It has the idea of being cut down in His prime, speaking of sacrifice or giving His best. Remember, this is not a stuffed toy lamb. The lamb is red with its own blood. It's a red, bloodied and murdered lamb. He was butchered as a beast bearing the murderous marks, the wicked wounds of the sacrificial slaughter. He is seen in heaven bloody and messy probably stretched upon the altar, violently maimed because of your sins and my sins.

This is the picture in heaven—a bleeding and bloody Lamb. With His Father, He is the centerpiece of heaven, and He is the content of the music sung there. This is reminiscent of when John the Baptist said, "Behold the Lamb" (see John 1:29). As I have said, John wasn't talking about Christ as a cuddly toy or pet you can possess, but the Passover Lamb who would be slaughtered on the Cross.

The words "worthy is the Lamb who was slain" call out to us, "Look at the Cross! Focus on the sacrificial Lamb, the sacrifice God provides!" The supreme depth of God's love for all humanity is so great that He gave His only beloved Son. He is the center of worship. Our songs of worship should be more about the Cross, the Lamb, the sacrifice and the blood instead of abstract vagaries. It's time we bring the Cross center-stage. The Cross should be in our architecture and in our media presentations. A survey was done at the Worship Institute of over 200 songs from various

*He was **butchered** as a beast bearing the **murderous** marks .*

publishers, churches and ministries. Of those 6% were about the redemption of Christ. This tells us where we are in our worship song content and focus.

Then the angels continued that the Lamb is worthy to "receive…" This word "receive" means to gain, to get or obtain. The Lamb deserves to get and obtain our worship and the worship of angels and elders and all creatures.

ATTRIBUTES AND ATTITUDES

Angels and their songs speak to us today. The Lamb they sing about gives us a model for our worship, as they sing a sevenfold tribute of the worthiness of the Lamb to receive *power, wealth, wisdom, strength, honor, glory and praise.*

Scholars say the first four words of this list speak of the attributes that belong to Christ—power, wealth, wisdom and strength. The last three (honor, glory, praise) relate more to an attitude toward Him. All the words are preceded by a single article making the whole list read as a seven-part word.

1. <u>Worthy is the Lamb who was slain to receive "power."</u>

Power is strength (or in the Greek, *dunamis* power.) It implies miracle-working power and speaks of the unlimited ability to perform. His power is enough to perform miracles. Nothing can withstand the force of His sovereign will. It also speaks of the power and resources that arise from armies of great numbers. To help us grasp the concept, consider the power of the unity of all our armed forces combined, advancing as one big force. The Word gives many examples insights into the strength and power of the Lord:

"Be exalted, O Lord, in Your own strength!
We will sing and praise Your power" (Ps. 21:13).

"Great is our Lord, and mighty in power" (Ps. 147:5).

"And Jesus came and spoke to them, saying, 'All authority [power] has been given to Me in heaven and on earth'" (Matt. 28:18).

2. <u>Worthy is the Lamb who was slain to receive "wealth."</u>

Wealth here means "abundance or plenitude of possessions." It means "being enriched or riches." To Him belong wealth, infinite resources and fullness of divine gifts. The Word is clear that wealth is not about having lots of money:

"Oh, the depth of the riches both of the wisdom and knowledge of God! How unsearchable are His judgments and His ways past finding out!" (Rom. 11:33).

"And my God shall supply all your need according to His riches in glory by Christ Jesus" (Phil. 4:19).

It is by the Lamb that we receive riches—fullness, fatness and enrichment.

3. <u>Worthy is the Lamb who was slain to receive "wisdom."</u>

Wisdom is supreme intelligence and mental excellence. "To know the highest ends and best means to their attainment" is what the word means. The Greek word is *sophia*. Worthy is He to receive wisdom.

"To God our Savior, who alone is wise, be glory and majesty, dominion and power, both now and forever. Amen" (Jude 25).

"Now to the King eternal, immortal, invisible, to God who alone is wise, be honor and glory forever and ever. Amen" (1 Tim. 1:17).

4. <u>Worthy is the Lamb who was slain to receive "strength."</u>

The angels are referencing the Lamb's might, ability and force. He is able to disarm any foe and conquer any enemy. There are no circumstances He cannot master.

> *"Oh Lord God of our fathers, are you not God in heaven, and do You not rule over all the kingdoms of the nations, and in Your hand is there not power and might so that no one is able to withstand You?" (2 Chron. 20:6).*

5. <u>Worthy is the Lamb who was slain to receive "honor."</u>

Now the "Angel Anthem" begins to reference *attitudes* of worship. Honor is deference or reverence belonging or shown to one because of high rank or office. This is the kind of honor we would give a five-star general. In other words, we give God the highest possible esteem of public distinction that can be conferred. Glory to God in the highest.

6. <u>Worthy is the Lamb who was slain to receive "glory."</u>

The Greek word is *doxa*, meaning "to ascribe honor and praise to God; to ascribe magnificence, excellence, preeminence, dignity, grace and majesty to Him." He is the King of majesty. To

Him belong all majesty and might as our most supreme Ruler. Glory is the majesty of God's absolute perfection—the absolutely perfect inward and personal excellence of Christ.

Often when we sing honor and glory to God, the words slide easily out of our mouths without our thinking much about it. But the honor and glory due God is rich with meaning. To go to another level in worship we must know of whom we sing and not be casual about Him.

7. <u>Worthy is the Lamb who was slain to receive "praise."</u>

The Greek word for praise is *eulogia*, meaning "laudation." It is also translated as "blessing." So the sevenfold proclamation is climaxed with the praise of Christ by virtue of who He is and what He has done.

Everything is rightfully His. He bought it and purchased it by dying on the Cross and rising from the dead. Therefore it calls forth grateful acknowledgement by all His subjects to give Him utmost blessing. He receives greatest praise because He earned it, He deserves it, He accomplished it, and He is worthy of it. He has the weight and substance to get it.

What did the people cry out when Jesus came into Jerusalem on the day of His Triumphal Entry? "Hosanna! Blessed is He who comes in the name of the Lord!" (Mark 11:9). If we do not praise the greatness and grandeur of God by revealing His character and attributes, then our worship remains low. Seeing how worship occurs on the other side keeps our worship high where it needs to be.

THE WONDER OF ANGELS

Someone once said, "Worship is the adoring response of the creature to the infinite majesty of God," This is so true. Worship is submission to Him and the soul's occupation with God Himself.

Are you occupied with God or are you occupied with all the peripherals? Maybe that's why leaders are burned out with the business of doing worship, planning, producing and practicing—all that we think is necessary for worship.

*Such devotion should become a **perpetual attitude** of the heart that permeates with heat for God until life **throbs** with the numinous, the **majestic**, and the **mysterious**.*

A story is told of a man who for many years had gone out into the streets and preached the gospel. Few people would gather to listen. Often he was made an object of scorn. When asked why he kept going when received with so little appreciation, he answered, "Oh, you don't understand, I am not here to please people. I am here to praise the Lord with the angels." You see he was plugged into the other side. He marched out, like David, when he heard the sound of angels marching in the tops of the trees! When the heavenly army goes out, the earthly army goes out. Such devotion should become a perpetual attitude of the heart that permeates with heat for God until life throbs with the numinous, the majestic, and the mysterious. This is the wonder of angels.

What is our response to the great, voluminous worship of the choir of angels? That our worship should be high, loud, full-bodied, full-spirited, full-throated, excited, exuberant, lavish and extravagant. A little "praise the Lord" won't do. Why do we stand there with hands at half-mast! (Did somebody die?) Run the flag all they way up the flagpole! He is risen! Put the other hand up as well!

The Lamb of God sits at the right hand of the Majesty on high. What we have read is the wonder of angels and the Lord Jesus Christ is at its center. Jesus sits next to Yahweh and He is the object of worship of heaven's angels. It is God we worship. We sing of His character, His attributes, His acts, and it is for His pleasure. The psalmist phrased it very well: "Praise the Lord, you his angels, you mighty ones who do his bidding, who obey his word. Praise the Lord, all his heavenly hosts [you troops and troops of armed forces, singing soldiers, celestial luminaries!], you his servants who do his will. Praise the Lord, all his works everywhere in his dominion. Praise the Lord, O my soul" (Ps. 103:20-22, NIV).

So here we come to a song of the angels, the mass choir of angels. Their worship is an example to us. The Holy Spirit is inviting us to sing their song from the other side. Lift up your heart and hands in worship to God as you sing:

"Worthy is the Lamb, who was slain,
to receive power and wealth and wisdom and strength
and honor and glory and praise!"

---

[1] Carl Boberg, 1886, "How Great Thou Art," Swedish melody arranged by Manna Music, 1955.

CHAPTER TEN

CREATION'S CRESCENDO

*And every creature which is in heaven and on the earth
and under the earth and such as are in the sea,
and all that are in them, I heard saying:*

*"Blessing and honor and glory and power
Be to Him who sits on the throne,
And to the Lamb, forever and ever!"*

*Then the four living creatures said, "Amen!" And the twenty-four
elders fell down and worshiped Him who lives forever and ever.
(Rev. 5:13, 14)*

Pierre Teilhard de Chardin said, "We are not human beings with a temporary spiritual experience; we are spirit beings having temporary human experience." Inside of each of us is a spirit man, an alien (someone who is not from around here.) When this body folds off like a dusty old garment and the maggots eat it away, only the spirit man will be left. The real you, not your earth-suit shell, will be worshipping in the presence of God. Worship as it occurs in heaven is our model as we think about our odyssey and ask God to take us further.

High-View Worship

It is believed that the early Christians sang songs from Revelation as doxologies because their grand lyrics reflect the spirit of adoration and represent the language of heaven. These songs are transcendent; they are older than humanity. They transcend time and space. This is important to understand because in a pop-cultural age of simulation and stimulation of sight and sound, we tend to have a virtual experience of worship where the experience, the production, the planning, the process and the performance get all the attention. Sometimes we never get past that to Jesus.

As we look into the picture of perfect worship in heaven, we get a high view of God. This raises our worship to another level. But low-view worship says, "I didn't get anything out of that," or "What song are you guys going to sing? I really like *those* songs—choose them because they come from my favorite artist." When we sing about what *we* like and want to receive, our worship becomes humanistic and consumer-driven. This kind of low worship becomes a "feel-good" that borders on sensuality. In contrast, when we hear songs from the other side, we can learn new ways to worship God. We begin to enter a dimension of worship similar to what the angels experience.

DIRT SUITS AND EARTH SUITS

When you were conceived in your mother's womb, you became a living soul. The real you cannot be seen, only the outer crust. So when it comes time to worship and you touch the transcendent, the real spirit-person inside comes alive. He is spiritual and salutes when you touch true spiritual worship. The outer person likes the "feel-good," the "rush," the stuff that flesh feels. That's fine for some things because we live in this human shell. But when it comes to real worship, we do so "in the Spirit...and have no confidence in the flesh" (Phil. 3:3). The inner spirit man hungers for supernatural worship.

John has a vision of the realm of angels, elders, aliens and animals. He sees all creation, all humans, all celestial and terrestrial creatures, cherubs, and seraphs worshipping.

A Gaze into the Other Side

John has a vision of the realm of angels, elders, aliens and animals. He sees all creation, all humans, all celestial and terrestrial creatures, cherubs, and seraphs worshipping. It's the unveiling of the real worship on the other side. It's an example of how we are to worship: "Blessing and honor and glory and power be to Him who sits on the throne, and to the Lamb, forever and ever!" is the cry of every creature. Let's delve into this magnificent, heavenly scene.

Wings, Whales and Worms

And every creature which is in heaven and on the earth and under the earth and such as are in the sea, and all that are in them (Rev. 5:13a).

"Every creature" means *all* creatures—any, each and every creature. The term is all-inclusive. The whole creation groans, as scholars say, waiting for the day when it will be set free from its bondage of decay and share in the magnificent liberty that belongs to the children of God. "For the creation was subjected to futility, not willingly, but because of Him who subjected it in hope; because the creation itself also will be delivered from the bondage of corruption into the glorious liberty of the children of God. For we know that the whole creation groans [makes a sound] and labors with birth pangs together until now" (Rom. 8:20-22). When I read this, I see creation resembling a bride who at the moment she was standing at the front of the church to be married saw her bridegroom die. She still is standing at the altar in her wedding dress, the beautiful woman creation, sobbing with her eyes full of tears. All creation, every creature "sobs," waiting to be set free.

Think about the vast number of creatures that must be in heaven. John says he sees and hears every creature in the vaulted expanse of the heavens—our starry sky and the universe beyond. The psalmist boldly proclaims: "The heavens will praise Your wonders, O Lord" (Ps. 89:5).

In addition to every creature in heaven, every creature on the earth sings creation's crescendo. This includes every animal on land—horses, dogs, camels, chickens, and wild beasts of all kinds. Can you imagine hearing a chorale of lions, llamas, and loons all harmonizing?

Imagine hearing a chorale of lions, llamas, and loons all harmonizing.

Those underneath the ground also sing. Not only does this crescendo of worship come from creatures of the sky and land but it also comes from the subterranean parts of the earth. This is a complete picture of total praise. Are these worms, maggots, serpents and moles that John hears worshipping the Lamb Lion? Or are these the dead, saved and unsaved, that rise up to worship in this creaturely crescendo? The answer is "Yes!"

Then creatures in the sea are heard singing. Whatever is on or in the oceans, lakes, rivers and streams sing—whales, salmon, shrimp, dolphin, turtles, and octopi. The sad fact is some Christians won't sing—what's up with that? A while back, I went to Alaska to catch some salmon. I praised Him there in the wild as I stepped into the 45-degree river and felt slippery salmon brush against my leg! We were all praising our Creator! "Let heaven and earth praise Him, *the seas and everything that moves in them*" (Ps. 69:34, italics added).

BIRDS, BEASTS, BUGS & BASS SING

I heard saying: "Blessing and honor and glory and power be to Him who sits on the throne, and to the Lamb, forever and ever!"
(Rev. 5:13b)

John heard the same affirmations and proclamations he heard earlier, only these were all the creatures alive and dead. Creatures with fins and wings, legs and tentacles arise with a loud crescendo and praise Him. (I am having a worship experience right now while I write this!)

All creatures were singing this word: "blessing." It means they were singing the laudation, the praise of God.

They were singing "honor" which means "having value." This is the kind of honor that gives recognition and reverence. It is conferring and giving rightful honor to His name.

"Glory" was the next word that the creatures of earth, sea and sky sang. This is the majesty, the splendor, and absolute perfection of God.

Then the lyric "power" was sung. This indicates God's might and dominion.

This fourfold ascription expresses the universality of this particular song. The divine doxology crescendos from the four corners of the earth, the great expanse of the heavens, and from departed spirits as well. Not only the living creatures (the worship leaders who initiated this worship), but also the twenty-four elders and the angels (the outer circle of an innumerable, an incalculable number) join in. All sing endlessly of His glory and His attributes. But now, from all corners of the earth, below and above the sky, worship culminates in a great crescendo of all creation to the Lion King, the Passover Lamb.

Creatures with *fins and wings, legs and tentacles* arise with *a loud crescendo and praise* Him.

The song continues, "Be to Him who sits on the throne, and to the Lamb." The One who sits on the throne is Yahweh—the I Am who I Am, Adonai—the Lord and Master, Jehovah—the AM, El Shaddai—the Almighty, and El-Elyon—the Most High. He is the

Great Potentate, the Everlasting One, the Ancient of Days, our heavenly Father. This is who sits on the throne.

But the creatures sing of the Lamb as well. Not a cute, white stuffed toy but the Lamb that was slaughtered and bloody. It's not a pretty picture but that is the centerpiece of our worship because Jesus Christ crucified is the focal point of heaven. He is the One in the center and before the throne, the Lion of the tribe of Judah who is also a Lamb.

The use of the word "be" underscores the continuum of the nature of God's qualities that follow. They are inseparable to His being. His qualities are not just *ascribed to* Him—He *is* those qualities.

FATHER AND SON

The close relationship between God and the Lamb comes out repeatedly in the Apocalypse. See how this song arises to praise the One on the throne and the Lamb—both equally worthy of worship and ruling in majesty. The importance of keeping the second Person of the Godhead (Jesus) in focus should not be dismissed.

John witnessed that Jesus is the image of the invisible God. He is the firstborn of all creation. He has fulfilled the purpose for which all things came into being and to which all things are moving in this odyssey. He is the A to Z of our lives; His identity as the Lamb continually keeps Him before us and reminds us of the centrality of

His work to redeem humankind. The Cross is at the center. We cannot come to God and worship except through the blood of His Son. And so when John the Baptist said, "Behold the Lamb of God!" (John 1:36), he was saying a profound statement. He was saying, "Behold the Cross! Behold the Passover Lamb! Behold the forgiveness of sins!"

CROSS CENTRAL

We must remember to keep Jesus and the Christ-event at the center of our worship. To see how far we have gone off course, go through your repertoire of last year's pop-songs. See how many songs you have sung about the Cross, or His blood, His Second Coming or the Resurrection. It is probably less than ten percent! There's the ancient mystery of God-centeredness that must be restored in our pop-culture music. It doesn't matter how you sing it, rap it, clap it, but your song has to be pregnant with good theology of the Christ-event. It has to proclaim Jesus, who is at the center, and El Shaddai, who sits on the throne.

BILLY GRAHAM WEEPS

There was a time early in Billy Graham's ministry when he was preaching to a great crowd in Dallas, Texas. Strangely enough, few people responded to his message. As he was leaving the platform, a dear old saint put his arm around him and said, "Billy, you didn't preach the Cross tonight." The great evangelist went immediately to his room and wept. Then he made a resolve before God: "O God, so help me, there will never be a sermon that I preach unless the cross is central."[1]

Worship leader, will you make a vow before God that you will never lead worship unless the Cross is central? Have we gotten away from the centerpiece of our worship by thinking it needs to have a good sound byte and a great "feel-good"? I know of an instance where a worship leader was practicing with the worship team and the tenor pointed out, "Hey, we're not singing any songs about Jesus; we're just singing poetic metaphors. Do you think we should be doing that?" Instead of agreeing, the worship leader fired the tenor on the spot and went ahead with what she planned. We have incorrect values in our worship philosophy. Worship leaders, as well as all leaders, should be grounded in the knowledge of God.

> *The insects that play in the sun and the bugs that work in the dirt all declare the glory of the Creator.*

The song concludes with "forever and ever!" The Amplified version says it this way: "through the eternities of the eternities!" We will praise Him forever, and all Creation will glorify Him forever who lives forever.

THE CREATURELY SYMPHONY

Then the four living creatures said, "Amen!" (Rev. 5:14a).

It was a custom in the synagogues when someone had read, spoken or offered up a prayer to God, that others would respond "Amen!" making the utterance their own. "Amen" is practically a universal word and has been called the best-known word in human speech. It means "I believe." "Faithful" is connected to that word. "Amen" means "sure" or "truly." It speaks of absolute trust and confidence. Unable to find the words to express any higher adoration, all living creatures simply just keep on saying "Amen! Amen! Amen!" So we should say "Blessing (Amen!), and honor (Amen!), and glory (Amen!), and power (Amen!)."

And the twenty-four elders fell down and worshiped Him who lives forever and ever (Rev. 5:14b).

At the end of the song the twenty-four elders respond. These elders are worshippers. As the cherubs continue their chanting of acclamations, these twenty-four counselors fall prostrate on the ground. They show obeisance by falling down and humbling themselves before Him who sits on the throne and the Lamb.

Jesus is ever living. It isn't just that He was alive and lived; but He lived and kept on living, and He once died, but now He is alive and He lives, lives, lives without end! He keeps on living, and He keeps on and keeps on and keeps on living—that is the picture here. Not only does God live eternally, He is the source of all life. He is at the center of all life, all molecular structures. With Him belongs absolutely all immortality; He lives forever and ever. Again our attention is turned to the ages of the ages, timeless ages.

The scene here of this awesome crescendo of worship by all of creation is full of devotion and theology. The worship by the animal kingdom is not dependent upon moods and cool musical grooves. We don't read here: "Well, I'm not in the mood to worship today!" said the chicken. The eagle doesn't say, "I'm too busy soaring right now." True worship comes from the heart of the contrite believer as well as from all creatures. This worship is far beyond the giddy praise of the outer court and what makes us feel good. There is no mention of us earthlings and our dysfunction in the songs from the other side because worship songs there are all about Him and not about us.

One of the most profound mystical passages on the sacred symphony of creation is in Psalm 148. In this universal anthem of creation no created animal is left out.

"Praise the Lord. Praise the Lord from the heavens, praise him in the heights above. Praise him, all his angels, praise him, all his heavenly hosts. Praise him, sun and moon, praise him, all you shining stars. Praise him, you highest heavens and you waters above the skies. Let them praise the name of the Lord, for he commanded and they were created. He set them in place forever and ever; he gave a decree that will never pass away.

Praise the Lord from the earth, you great sea creatures and all ocean depths, lightning and hail, snow and clouds, stormy winds that do his bidding, you mountains and all hills, fruit trees and all cedars, wild animals and all cattle, small creatures and flying birds, kings of the earth and all nations, you princes and all rulers on earth, young men and maidens, old men and children.

Let them praise the name of the Lord, for his name alone is exalted; his splendor is above the earth and the heavens" (Ps.148:1-13, NIV).

This song in Psalms calls the universe to thunder praise, and in Revelation the universe is actually doing it. The hills, the streams, the flood, the birds, whales and the beasts that roam over the earth worship God. The insects that play in the sun and the bugs that work in the dirt all declare the glory of the Creator. Every knee will bow before Him (in heaven, on the earth, under the earth and in the sea) and every tongue will "confess that Jesus Christ is Lord, to the glory of God the Father" (Phil. 2:11).

The universal dimension of heaven's worship is breathtaking. No creature is left out. Those of all shapes and sizes, ugly and beautiful, legged and finned, exalt the One who made them. Why would we want sing our little plastic songs among those who look just like us? There is no "ghetto worship" in heaven, rather a polyphony of diversity.

The Lord made the heavens; splendor and majesty are before Him. Strength and joy are in His presence. Ascribe to the Lord, oh families of nations, ascribe to the Lord glory and strength. Ascribe to the Lord the glory due His name. Bring an offering and come before Him and worship the Lord in the splendor of His holiness. Tremble before Him, all the earth. The world is firmly established, it cannot be moved. Let the heavens rejoice, let the earth be glad, let them say upon the nations, "The Lord reigns!"

All creation is guided to its destination of heavenly worship on the other side.

Praise God from whom all blessings flow
Praise Him all creatures here below
Praise Him above you heavenly hosts
Praise Father, Son, and Holy Ghost[2]

---

[1] Billy Graham, "Evangelism Message and Method", *Christianity Today*, III no. 22 (August 1959).

[2] Louise Bourgeois and Ken Thomas, "Doxology," Public Domain